ARE YOU A SHY PERSON?

DID YOU KNOW THAT:

- Forty percent of the population believes they are shy.

- Shyness is a *temporary* emotional reaction triggered by encountering new people and situations.

- Some people have a genetic predisposition to shyness.

- Shy people aren't "unsociable." They are their own worst critics.

- Shyness is curable?

CONQUERING SHYNESS

From its causes to its cure, from cognitive therapy to the "nuts and bolts" of planning small talk and learning how to write your own script, you can learn to feel confident and at ease in any situation. Quizzes, exercises, case histories, and a personal diary that charts your progress are all part of an innovative battle plan guaranteed to win!

CONQUERING
SHYNESS

THE BATTLE ANYONE CAN WIN

JONATHAN M. CHEEK, M.D.

AND BRONWEN CHEEK

WITH LARRY ROTHSTEIN

A DELL TRADE PAPERBACK

A DELL TRADE PAPERBACK
Published by
Dell Publishing
a division of
Bantam Doubleday Dell Publishing Group, Inc.
666 Fifth Avenue
New York, New York 10103

*This book is dedicated to
all the people who
have participated in
our research on shyness.*

Acknowledgments

Many people became involved in the life of this book. Thank you to Ken Rivard, for providing valuable editorial input at various stages of the project. Thanks go to all the psychologists who have collaborated in the research on shyness, especially Arnold Buss and Lisa Melchior.

Fred Mansbridge, Tricia Waters, and Timothy Cheek provided support, guidance, and unfailing belief that saw us through more than one frustrating episode in the writing process.

Friends who generously gave their time to and insightful comments on the manuscript much improved the book: Margery Lucas, Keith Lewinstein, Robin Akert, Jean Jacobsen, Kathryn Jacobsen, and Pat McAfee. Molly Jones kindly allowed us use of her wonderful printer and access to the copier.

Last, and certainly not least, thank you to our friends who innocently asked, "How's the book going?" and with infinite patience and kindness listened to a longer answer than the question deserved.

Contents

Introduction

In 1977 I entered graduate school at the University of Texas with only a vague hint of the specific area of psychology I wanted to study. If pressed, I'd say that the subject of anxiety interested me. During that first semester my vague hint evolved into certainty.

I was enrolled in a seminar on social psychology that met twice a week in the afternoon. The format was typical: A professor lectured twelve students seated around a long table; discussion centered on individual research topics. None of us had trouble digging up background material or hammering a presentation together, but for a few of my classmates standing up in front of peers and making a presentation was a trial by fire. The one I can't forget was a woman I'll call Dana. For her, the very idea of being the focus of everyone's attention, even for a brief period of time, opened a very deep vein of anxiety.

I remember her standing behind her chair. A tall, attractive woman with shoulder-length brown hair, she eyed her notes nervously, gulped once, and plunged in. Her hair hung down like a curtain on either side of her face, and almost immediately students began to ask her to speak louder. As she gained a bit of confidence, her voice became more audible—but I noticed that while she used her right hand to turn the pages of her notes, her left hand continually massaged her throat. For the entire twenty-minute talk, her left hand remained at her neck, steadily massaging up and down as if this action was necessary for her to speak at all. As she spoke, I lost the thread of her topic. The excruciating spectacle of her discomfort drove the significance of her words right out of my head. When at last her presentation came to an end, she sank back into her seat, letting her hands fall to her sides. To this day I can't recall Dana's topic, but indelibly etched in my memory is the sight of her neck raw and red—she looked as though someone had been trying to strangle her.

Dana's problem set my mind working. Here was a very bright young woman—a degree candidate in one of the top ten psychology programs in the country, a student who had obviously spent a great deal of time preparing and organizing her talk—and yet she seemed so obviously handicapped I wondered if she'd make it through graduate school. Well, I thought, trying to put her out of my mind, obviously she's shy—as if that explained everything.

At odd moments over the next few days, Dana's image would come to me. I'd be having a beer or reading when suddenly the vision of her rubbing her throat would interrupt me. *Why* was she shy? Does everyone experience shyness the same way? Was Dana simply more susceptible to shyness than the rest of us, her classmates? Was her problem connected with how she had been brought up or had she just been born shy?

Eventually, my curiosity got the better of me. I went over to the library and searched through research journals trying to find some answers to these questions. Surely someone before me had wondered about problems like Dana's and done some studies on this topic. Yet, after hours of tracking down a few references, I discov-

ered that there was little research on shyness—and much conten-
tion about it.

Researchers couldn't even agree on a definition for it. Shyness
was usually lumped together with other agreed-upon personality
traits such as *introversion* or *general anxiety*. In the clinical literature, which deals with actual case histories, I found a similar reluctance to recognize shyness as a problem in and of itself. For the
typical clinical psychologist, shyness was merely a symptom of an
underlying neurosis or psychosis. Take care of those and the symptom would vanish.

This lack of attention to shyness had a deleterious effect for one
simple reason: *If there's no problem, there's no cure.* In other words,
until psychologists agreed that shyness was a problem in its own
right, until they took a close look at its mechanisms, they couldn't
begin to devise treatments for it. For psychologists shyness had
always been a little of this, a little of that. In other words, it fell
through the cracks—and so did Dana.

Until 1977. In that year a California social psychologist named
Philip Zimbardo published people's responses to a very simple
question he'd been asking since the early seventies: *Are you a shy
person?* [1]

The response, to put it mildly, was overwhelming. Extrapolat-
ing from his survey, Zimbardo estimated that almost forty percent
of the American population would have answered "yes" to his
question. Zimbardo's query opened the door to the study of shyness. Any topic that got that kind of response—even if nobody
could quite agree what it meant—deserved a lot more attention.

Thanks to Dana and Zimbardo, I decided I would study shyness.

A logical way to begin was to examine some of the assumptions
psychologists had been making about shyness. They often catego-
rized shy people as unsociable, for example, implying that shy
people weren't interested in being friendly. I devised a questionnaire to divide students who described themselves as shy from
those who did not. [2] I introduced pairs of unacquainted students
(one shy, one not shy) and left them alone for five minutes with

instructions to "get to know one another." Afterward, questioning the students on their brief conversation, I discovered several things:

First of all, shy people aren't unsociable. Again and again, the shy participants told me that they *wanted* to make friends, but a barrier of anxiety prevented them from being as friendly as they would have liked.

Secondly, the shy students rated their performance much more harshly than did a panel of objective observers (who didn't know who was shy and who wasn't). Shy people were obviously their own worst critics.

Finally, although I'd selected shy participants based on their reports of physical symptoms of shyness or their belief that they lacked social skills, some of them said later that thinking about their shyness was in fact the worst part of their experience.

As I continued my research, I saw that I needed to measure not just one overall experience of shyness, but three specific areas. I had to refine my questioning to include physical symptoms, thoughts and worries, and behaviors.[3] Some shy people were mostly concerned with physical symptoms—with blushing, a racing heartbeat, and the like; others were troubled by negative thoughts and worries. Still others bemoaned their lack of social skills. Many suffered from more than one of these three types of symptoms. As my research made clear to me, shyness came in many guises.

Shyness was a *syndrome,* a complex of symptoms that differed from individual to individual. Using a method designed to combat the physical symptoms of shyness can't help the person with a critic inside his head telling him that he's a social flop. Likewise, practicing social skills won't put an end to the butterflies in someone's stomach. Effective treatment would require specific measures and therapies tailored to the individual's type of shyness.

In stepping through the doorway that Zimbardo opened, I've spent many hours happily immersed in finding out all that I can about shyness. In 1983 shyness began reaping national attention when I presented a new study demonstrating the genetic component of shyness.[4] I thought the clamor over shyness would quickly fade. But it didn't. As the years went by I continued to be called by newspaper and magazine writers for interviews, and by therapists wanting to know the latest research on treatments for shyness.

Not so long ago the sum total of all shyness research would hardly have filled a magazine article, let alone a whole book. A graduate student wanting to know about shyness today would have no difficulty finding research on it.[5] Over the last ten years my own research, and that of other psychologists, has led to new knowledge. And each new bit of knowledge about shyness has led to better methods for overcoming it.

It's time that you, the everyday shy person, had access to this new knowledge. As you can see in the fact list below, there are many facets to shyness:

- Shyness is a temporary emotional reaction triggered by encountering new people and situations.
- Shyness often becomes an integral part of a person's identity and a "reason" for retreating from the social world.
- Some people have a genetic predisposition to shyness.
- Physical symptoms of shyness can include blushing, sweating, shaking, or an increased heart rate.
- Shy people tend to have low self-esteem and are preoccupied with the thought that they're socially inadequate.
- Shy people are their own worst critics, demanding phenomenally high standards of performance for themselves.
- Shyness has a behavioral aspect—some shy people simply don't know what to say or do in social situations.
- Shy people are often lonely. They have fewer close friends and date less frequently than non-shy people.
- Shy people earn less money and have more difficulty advancing their careers.

Don't let this list daunt you. No one is doomed to life as a shy person. If you're tired of being a shrinking violet, read on. In the following chapters I'll help you determine your type of shyness and understand the latest research on it. Armed with that information and the practical steps you can take to overcome shyness, you can design your own personal program to enable you to abandon your life as a wallflower. Throughout the book you'll also find accounts of shyness from shy people themselves. Of course, their names and certain details have been changed to protect their privacy.

Overcoming shyness can feel like a war with yourself. But it's a battle you *can* win.

THE
BASICS
OF
OVERCOMING
YOUR
SHYNESS

CHAPTER 1

Understanding Your Shyness

The lush green enclave of Wellesley College, with its well-manicured lawns and pastoral atmosphere, seems designed to discourage shyness. The stress and menace of gritty urban campuses seem far away. The peaceful landscape would seem to encourage even the most reticent wallflower to step forward and flourish.

Appearances can be deceiving, however. Five years ago Wellesley asked me to help organize a shyness-support group. Even students as talented and privileged as the young women who attend this prestigious school wrestle with shyness, as their comments illustrate:

Chris: "When I was a child, I'd cry when people would try to talk to me. Later I quit kindergarten because of it. Now here I am in college, and whether I'm in my dorm or in class, I still blush and my heartbeat goes wild whenever I speak to other people. I'm always so preoccupied with these physical characteristics that I can't think of anything else."

Linda: "I became especially aware of my shyness when I was in high school. I didn't have very many friends and I spent most of my time alone. To this day I have trouble talking with people comfortably because I'm always so self-conscious, and I know that a lot of this comes from low self-esteem. I worry about the impression I'm making on other people."

Joanne: "I just don't know what to say to people—you know, how to start a conversation. When I'm around a group of people I find myself staring at the floor. I wish I could make small talk or tell a joke, but I can't ever think of anything interesting to say."

These three people describe shyness in three very different ways. Chris says she's been shy since she was a small child and that she's mainly troubled by physical symptoms. Linda first became aware of her shyness during adolescence, and feels that much of her shyness comes from her feelings of low self-esteem; she worries about what other people will think of her. And Joanne attributes her shyness to a lack of social skills.

Are all three of them really shy? Yes. Even though each describes her problem differently, all of them are shy. That's because shyness isn't one single response to social situations. Shyness is a syndrome, a complex interaction of feelings, thoughts, and behavior.[1] You may be a blusher or you may be a worrier, or you may be both. And whether you're a blusher or a worrier, you may also feel that you lack social skills.

WHAT'S YOUR SHYNESS QUOTIENT?

One day after teaching a class on shyness, I met with one of my freshman students in my office. Susan told me she considered herself "closet shy," explaining that to her friends back home she was seemingly outgoing, but in reality she felt shy in a number of situations. Specifically, she told me she was having a rough time making new friends in college. With utter frustration Susan exclaimed, "Professor Cheek, it's almost impossible for me to meet new people, or to show someone I'm interested in them. How can

I be relaxed in some situations and a complete wallflower in others?"

I explained to her that there wasn't anything wrong with her, that there are different degrees of shyness. There are some people who feel shy just about all the time—even with their own family members—and there are other people, like herself, who feel shy only in certain situations. And while shyness is usually only a temporary reaction, it does have predictable triggers. As I listed those triggers, Susan nodded her head in agreement with almost every one: Strangers. New social situations. Authority figures. Members of the opposite sex.

Perhaps you feel shy confronting a salesperson, a doctor, or your boss. Or maybe it's just meeting that attractive new employee at the office that sends you ducking down the hall in the opposite direction. Whatever sends your shyness quotient zooming, you'll get an indication of the intensity of your shyness in the following exercise.

RATING YOUR SHYNESS QUOTIENT

Instructions: Read each statement carefully and decide to what extent it is typical of your feelings and behavior. Fill in the blank next to each item by writing in a number from the scale below.

1 very uncharacteristic or untrue; strongly disagree
2 uncharacteristic
3 neutral
4 characteristic
5 very characteristic or true; strongly agree

_____ I'm tense when I'm with people I don't know well.
_____ It's difficult for me to ask other people for information.
_____ I'm often uncomfortable at parties and other social functions.
_____ When in a group of people, I have trouble thinking of the right things to say.
_____ It takes me a long time to overcome my shyness in new situations.
_____ It's hard for me to act natural when I'm meeting new people.

_____ I'm nervous when speaking to someone in authority.
_____ I have doubts about my social competence.
_____ I have trouble looking someone right in the eye.
_____ I feel inhibited in social situations.
_____ I find it hard to talk to strangers.
_____ I am more shy with members of the opposite sex.

Now add up your score. If you scored over 45, you're very shy. If your score is between 31 and 45, you're somewhat shy. If you scored below 31, you're probably not a particularly shy person, although you may feel shy in one or two situations. Most shy people score over 35, and a few reach the highest possible score of 60.[2]

You may find yourself thinking, "I'm more shy than I thought. I'll never be happy." Not so. The important lesson to learn from this exercise is that the more shy you are, the more patient you'll have to be with yourself; you've got a bigger task in front of you than someone who is only a little bit shy.

No matter how you scored on this exercise, however, you can take comfort in knowing that you're not alone. Studies reveal that _between 80 and 96 million Americans are shy._[3] Four out of every ten of us admits to some degree of shyness: Four out of every ten people in the checkout line at the supermarket; two-fifths of the members of your church group; forty percent of your fellow employees. All shy.

Or think of it this way: Only seven percent of Americans say they have _never_ experienced shyness!

WHAT KIND OF SHY PERSON ARE YOU?

To overcome your shyness you need to know more than just how shy you are. You need to narrow down the source of your problem by determining which group you fall into: Are you a shy person with physical distress, anxious thoughts and worries, or concern over the absence of social skills?

As you answer the questions below, imagine yourself in the social situation that makes you feel most shy. You might be on a date, at a party, or in the middle of introductions at a new job. In your mind's eye see yourself as vividly as possible and ask yourself: Am I blushing, sweating, or trembling? Am I worrying about the impression I'm making on others? Am I avoiding eye contact, staring at my feet?

YOUR SHYNESS TYPE

Instructions: Each cluster of shyness symptoms is described below. Read each type, then circle the answer to the question that follows.

- *Physical Distress*
  Butterflies in the stomach, a pounding heart, blushing, increased pulse, a dry mouth, sweating, or trembling. Any general physical tenseness and uneasiness.

Physical distress is an aspect of my shyness:

1. Never
2. Rarely
3. Sometimes
4. Usually
5. Always

- *Anxious Thoughts and Worries*
  Thinking about the situation you're in (for example, how terrible it is, or that you want to leave); being concerned with what others may be thinking about you and with the impression you are making; feeling generally insecure or self-conscious.

Anxious thoughts and worries are an aspect of my shyness:

1. Never
2. Rarely
3. Sometimes
4. Usually
5. Always

- *Absence of Social Skills*
  Observable actions that indicate to others that you're feeling shy—nervous gestures, difficulty speaking, inability to make eye contact, or simply avoiding interacting with others.

Absence of social skills is an aspect of my shyness:

1. Never   4. Usually
2. Rarely   5. Always
3. Sometimes

Now rank your shyness symptoms. People often have symptoms from each group, but rarely are the symptoms from different groups equally strong. If you circled the same number for two of the descriptions (or even all three), think long and hard, then re-rank each category.

1 = most severe   2 = next most severe   3 = least severe

Physical Distress   ＿＿＿
Anxious Thoughts/Worries   ＿＿＿
Absence of Social Skills   ＿＿＿

How did you score? Which area of shyness troubles you most? Do you have only one area of shyness that bothers you or more than one? Over half of the shy people who have filled out this questionnaire rank anxious thoughts and worries as their primary shyness symptom; the rest are evenly divided between those who cite physical distress and absence of social skills. And most shy people say that more than one type of symptom is a problem for them at least some of the time.[4] If you're troubled by more than one symptom of shyness, tackle your worst symptom first, then work on your next most troubling symptom.

Frequently in the course of this book I ask you to step back and take a critical look at yourself. My aim isn't to make you more judgmental—it's to improve the accuracy of your self-perception. Each time you force yourself to come up with a specific answer to one of my questions you add shape and color to your shyness. Your shyness begins to take a definite form; perhaps for the first time, you'll be able to "see" your shyness. Accuracy and detail lead to successful change. "When I meet members of the opposite sex I get butterflies in my stomach and my hands sweat" is a far more valuable self-evaluation than "I'm shy with new people." In the first instance, a specific situation is identified, with specific types of people. Consequently, you're on the way to creating a program that's targeted to your exact symptoms and situation. The second observation is so vague it's useless.

LATE- VS. EARLY-DEVELOPING SHYNESS

At the beginning of this chapter, Chris related that she'd felt shy ever since she was a small child, and that her symptoms of shyness were predominantly physical. She's an early-developing shy person. Linda, however, who began to feel shy during her teenage years, is a late-developing shy person.

The distinction between early- and late-developing shyness is important because different symptoms usually apply to each one.[5] Early-developing shyness occurs in people born with a highly sensitive nervous system. In such people physical arousal is the typical reaction to new or stressful situations. Remember that Chris said she used to cry whenever people tried to talk to her: Her nervous system overreacted to new people and places. Although Chris no longer cries when meeting new people, she's "adapted" by becoming a blusher with a pounding heartbeat. It's not surprising that Chris still feels shy today—there's strong evidence that early-developing shyness has a genetic component (more about that in Chapter 2).

During the stormy teenage years we begin to form our adult identity, and our self-esteem takes a roller-coaster ride. This is the period when Linda began feeling her shyness. While it's difficult to find a teenager who isn't shy at one time or another, most teenagers who were *not* shy as young children do outgrow this adolescent timidity. Sometimes, though, as in Linda's case, shyness persists into adult years. Our self-esteem continues to ride the roller-coaster and we keep evaluating our social dexterity. Shyness sets in, and preoccupation with how others perceive us becomes the focus of our social interactions.

Look back at how you ranked your type of shyness. Do you experience more of the physical symptoms of shyness? Are you an early-developing shy person? Are anxious thoughts and worries your main trouble? Are you a late-developing shy person?

About half of all shy adults have been shy all their lives, and the other half became shy in early adolescence. But suppose you ranked physical distress and anxious thoughts and worries pretty closely. How do you decide if you're an early- or late-developing shy person?

Try to recall the first time you felt shy. How old were you? You might want to ask your parents or other family members whether they remember you being shy as a toddler. If your first memories of shyness are before the age of eight, and especially if you're plagued by the physical symptoms of shyness, then you're an early-developing shy person. If, however, your first memories of shyness occurred between the ages of eight and fourteen, then you're a late-developing shy person.

IS IT REALLY WORTH THE EFFORT?

All right. You've identified your shyness symptoms and you know how shy you are compared to other people. Now comes the big decision: Are you ready to give up the shy life?

Are you ready to take a deep breath and begin making changes?

Are you willing to devote your time, energy, and courage to the exercises in this book?

Are you prepared to brush off small defeats with the knowledge that success will follow?

You can stop right here if you want. You can use the understanding you've gained so far about your shyness and simply say to yourself, "Well, I know more about my shyness now than I did before. I understand myself a little bit better. I'm content with that."

That's fine, but first think about five facts of life you'll be contending with if you choose to remain on the sidelines.

Number 1: The human need to be with others. We're a social species. Take a look around. How many times have you watched couples strolling down the street hand in hand? How many times have you seen two friends so engrossed in their conversation that they aren't aware of what's going on around them? How many times have you wished you were a part of the group sharing laughter over a summer's picnic or envied their shouts of glee as they race past one another on the ski slope? We really enjoy being with other people.[6] And, yet, we also fear other people. Our fear of strangers *is* adaptive; not everyone out there has good intentions toward us. Although we can't trust everyone who crosses our path, if we refuse to open up at all, we're sentenced to a life of isolation. It can't always be the other person who says the first hello, who makes the first overtures of friendship. Sometimes *you* must take the initiative, shy or not.

Number 2: The American culture's increasing impersonality. As a nation, we've changed a great deal since World War II, moving from the personal and familiar to the abstract and impersonal. We've become a highly mobile and competitive society made up of the nuclear family and, increasingly, single-parent families. It's no wonder sociologist Vance Packard describes our country as a "nation of strangers." Gone are the days of the extended family network, small-town community, and a work life devoted to one employer. Shyness may not be any more prevalent now than it was a generation or two ago, but today you must confront new situations and people with a regularity undreamed of by your grandparents. Unlike life on a farm or in a small town, our demanding and impersonal urban existence does little to accommodate us. Sink or swim is the usual attitude—and all too often shy people sink.

Number 3: The medical consequences of loneliness. It's a fact that shy people are lonelier than their more outgoing peers. In *The Broken Heart,* James Lynch asserts that "social isolation and chronic loneliness are significant contributors to premature death."[7] Later researchers don't always agree with this statement, but they do agree that loneliness can have deleterious health consequences.

When we feel lonely, we might try to drink away our "blues" or we may just become depressed in our isolation. Both alcohol and depression can make you more vulnerable to physical illness. This doesn't mean you should be alarmed about ever spending time alone—enjoying your own company is a different experience from thinking to yourself, "I'm lonely."

Number 4: Shyness won't disappear by itself. Zach, one of my study participants, told me, "Back to the first grade I can remember at recess time all the other kids playing on the school grounds. I stood by the flagpole alone and watched, too shy to join in. Things haven't changed much." Zach's lifelong problem with shyness isn't unique. In one of my studies I measured how lonely college students felt at the beginning and end of the semester. The non-shy students got to know their classmates and felt less lonely by the end of the school term. The shy students still felt lonely at the end of the semester.[8] Researchers at the Dallas Child Guidance Clinic conducted a follow-up study with shy children and found that sixteen to twenty-seven years later most continued to be quiet and retiring.[9] Overcoming early-developing shyness requires active intervention. It won't fade away on its own.

Number 5: The worst problem of all—being misunderstood. You've heard it a million times before: "Relax, you'll have a great time at this party—just be yourself . . ." "Oh, don't sweat the interview, just show 'em you know your stuff . . ." "If I'm late, have a drink and wait for me at the bar . . ." If only your friends knew how awkward and uncomfortable you feel in a roomful of noisy strangers, how tongue-tied you become during a job interview, and what a sore thumb you feel like sitting alone at a bar. Your friends may not understand your shyness. All they see is the person they know and like. Maybe you're a little "quiet," they think; it shouldn't be a problem—you can handle any social situation. The people who *don't* know you see something else. They wonder why you're so unfriendly. Maybe you're a snob, they think, so they pass you by. Maybe you're a pushover: The extroverts press their advantage and dominate conversations, impress the most attractive dating partners, cut into lines, get the promotions at work. In a rough-and-tumble world it isn't easy getting sympathy and help from those who don't understand shyness.[10] It's painful to be misunderstood.

Think about what I've just told you. Which seems more difficult: living with shyness or taking steps to overcome it? It takes vast amounts of energy (not to mention frustration) just coping with life as a shy person. Why not channel that energy into becoming a more confident and outgoing person?

Now take a deep breath, gather your courage, and let's begin building your program for overcoming shyness.

How to Use This Book

I've divided this book into two parts. In Part I, The Basics of Overcoming Your Shyness, you'll find the chapters related to your specific symptoms. In Part II, Applying Your New Confidence to Your Social Life, I talk about writing scripts and the broader issues of shyness as they pertain to friendships, romance, and careers.

If you're an early-developing shy person, and you're plagued with the physical symptoms of shyness, Chapter 2 is for you. Even if you're not particularly troubled by physical symptoms, I think you'll find the relaxation exercises in Chapter 2 helpful for quieting down your unrelenting internal critic. Chapters 3 and 4 are addressed to late-developing shy people—the anxious worriers. And everyone can turn to Chapter 5 to brush up on social skills.

But before you jump ahead, I'm going to insist that you do two things. First, you must do the exercises in the appropriate chapters. I wish I could say that just reading this book would magically make your shyness disappear, but you and I both know better. You've got to do the exercises and practice, practice, practice. Concentrate on each exercise without worrying about what comes next. One small step at a time should be your aim.

Second, you must set goals. Setting goals—*realistic goals*—can mean the difference between success and defeat. Without goals, you're likely to get frustrated and give up. But with proper goal-setting, you progress a little bit each day, improving at a pace that is comfortable for you.

THE GEOGRAPHY OF SHYNESS

Remember my student Susan who felt shy in some situations but not in others? Each of you has your own shyness situations, too. In the following exercise you're going to identify your personal shyness triggers. Take your time doing this, because the results are going to be important to all the other exercises you'll do further on. In later chapters you'll refer back to this exercise and use it for setting up your goals.

YOUR SHYNESS SITUATIONS

Instructions: Read each statement below and imagine yourself in the situation described. Are you feeling shy? How are you reacting? What are you doing? Place a check mark next to the statements that describe one of your shyness situations. In the space following the statement, *note your typical reaction* (i.e., pounding heart, anxious thoughts, etc.) to that situation. Don't let this list limit you—be sure to add any of your own shyness situations that don't appear on my list.

I feel shy when . . .

☐ being introduced to someone, in- _____
troducing myself, or introducing
someone I know to another person.

☐ expressing my opinions, talking _____
about myself and my interests.

☐ talking to people in authority _____
(i.e., supervisor, teacher, doctor).

☐ meeting people for the first time. _____

☐ at a social event where most peo- _____
ple are strangers.

☐ speaking up in a group situation. _____

☐ talking on the phone, especially with people I don't know. _____

☐ asking a sales clerk for help. _____

☐ interviewing for a job. _____

☐ talking to someone I'm attracted to. _____

☐ I'm around very popular, powerful, or attractive people. _____

☐ going out alone. _____

☐ I'm trying to keep a conversation going. _____

☐ I'm left alone with a new friend or date. _____

☐ getting ready to go out somewhere. _____

☐ receiving a compliment. _____

☐ meeting a new boss or supervisor. _____

☐ speaking in front of more than one or two people. _____

☐ starting a new job. _____

☐ trying to get to know someone better. _____

☐ shopping alone. _____

☐ riding on the bus or subway. _____

☐ making eye contact. _____

☐ I'm about to be evaluated. _____

☐ the situation calls for assertive behavior. _____

☐ I'm expected to be the host or hostess at a party. _____

☐ I want to say no. _____

☐ I see an acquaintance in a public place. _____

☐ I'm on a date. _____

Add your own "I feel shy when. . . ." situations here, describing your *typical* reactions to each of them.

Now go back and rank each situation from most fearful to least fearful, numbering your most fearful situation 1, the next most fearful 2, and so on, until you've ranked all of them. When you've finished, you'll have a good picture of your shyness situations. As you work on the exercises in later chapters and refer back to this list, you'll always want to begin with the situation that's least fearful for you.

As part of the program in this book you'll be keeping a notebook. I suggest you label it "Self-Development Notebook." It's for your eyes only. To protect your privacy, you may want to complete all the exercises in your notebook—even the ones that have writing space after them in the chapters. (Then you can leave your copy of this book out without being concerned that someone might pick it up, flip through it, and see what you've written.) A good way to begin your notebook is by writing down, in order, your shyness situations from the exercise above.

GOALS—A KEY TO SUCCESSFULLY CONQUERING SHYNESS

An important part of the exercises in each chapter is setting goals for yourself. Write your goals in your self-development notebook, keeping track of your thoughts and feelings as you go along. As the months go by, you can look back in your notebook and cheer yourself on with the gains you've made.

Since setting goals is a critical ingredient to overcoming your shyness, no matter what kind of shy person you are, you must learn how to set specific goals. This means becoming a rigorous observer of yourself. The chapters that address particular aspects of the shyness syndrome take for granted your ability to master this skill. Some of the steps will seem tedious, even silly, but until the system becomes second nature, *you must follow the steps exactly as I've outlined them below.*

1. Identify your goal.
2. Observe your "baseline" behavior—the way you currently think and act.
3. Divide your large goal into a series of smaller, manageable steps.
4. Attach numbers to each of these steps so that you can track your progress.
5. Reward yourself for each successfully completed step.

Reduced to an outline, goal-setting is disarmingly simple. Don't be deceived. Making the system work requires you to be a keen observer of your own behavior (which may be a completely new experience) and to balance your aspirations with your immediate level of anxiety.[11]

Let's look at the process in concrete terms. Sam is a shy, twenty-four-year-old computer programmer who's recently changed jobs. On most days, he quietly eats his lunch with a group of coworkers at a large table in his company's cafeteria. Although surrounded by obviously friendly people, he rarely exchanges more than a few words with his fellow diners.

What is Sam's goal? (Step 1) Sam very much wants to be a part of the lunchtime crowd, able to converse easily with his coworkers. He records this goal in his notebook.

How does Sam currently act and think during lunch? (Step 2) This is a far more difficult question to answer. For one thing, it requires Sam to play detective with himself at a time when he's likely to feel most uncomfortable. Sam knows enough to recognize that simply writing "I feel shy during lunch" is far too vague to be helpful. But at least the relaxation exercises in Chapter 2 have enabled him to calm down enough to begin asking himself important questions. *How* exactly does his shyness manifest itself? Does he have physical symptoms? If so, what are they? Maybe his shyness has more to do with his thought processes than actual physical symptoms. What is he thinking during lunch? When exactly do his physical symptoms/thoughts/feelings show themselves—as soon as he enters the cafeteria, when somebody says hello, when he's asked a question?

Sam asks himself these same questions on several different occasions, comparing his answers on different days, until a pattern begins to emerge. He notices, for example, that his hands and feet begin to sweat whenever George, his department supervisor, says hello. These symptoms escalate into an attack of heart palpitations and dryness in his mouth when he considers having a conversation with Kathy, the clever young programmer who was hired at the same time as Sam.

Observing yourself can be time-consuming and frustrating, but it's not a step you can skip. Sam, the ideally motivated shy person, faithfully records all his observations in his self-development notebook.

Next Sam breaks down his goal into manageable steps. (Step 3) Generally speaking, the key is not to bite off more than you can chew. Adhering to the motto "one small step at a time," Sam breaks down his long-range goal into short-term ones, prioritizes them (Step 4), and records them in his notebook. Here are the goals he sets for his first week.

At lunch this week:

1. On Monday I'll say hello to George before he greets me.
2. On each of the remaining days I'll greet one other person by name.
3. On Friday I'll ask Kathy how she's doing on that new software project.

Sam's goals during his first week may seem dishearteningly unambitious. Not so. Sam's smaller steps are very specific and targeted directly toward the larger goal of participating freely and easily in conversation during the shared lunch hour. He's wisely structuring his large goal out of small steps that lie within his grasp. If his program proves too easy, he always has the option of setting tougher objectives. People who set unreachable goals, either in hope of speeding the process up or whipping themselves into shape, often quit in frustration. If a goal proves unworkable, regard it as a problem in strategy rather than a judgment on your skill—it simply means you have to break down the unworkable step into smaller tasks. Sam's third step, for example, is probably a bit premature, given how shy he feels around Kathy. If so, he can make his approach more gradually.

Sam rewards himself frequently. (Step 5) At the end of his first day he decides to reward himself with a stop at his favorite record shop to splurge on two new compact discs. This is a big reward, to compensate him for finally getting off his duff and doing some real work to understand and conquer his shyness. After his big "first-day" reward, Sam's rewards for completing his daily goals are much smaller, usually just a mental pat on the back. At home each evening, he carefully records his progress in his self-development notebook. After completing his first week, he gives himself a Saturday off, doing whatever he wants (no chores or errands!) for successfully meeting his daily goals for one whole week.

Rewards can be anything that give you pleasure and enjoyment. A new book, a record, seeing a movie, for example, are appropriate rewards for completing one of the small steps toward your larger goal. Save your big treats, things you rarely indulge in, for big accomplishments. Whether it's dinner at an expensive restaurant or a weekend in the country, make your big rewards count.

With a successful week under his belt, Sam moves on to injecting himself into the lunchtime conversation. Over the weekend he writes out his new goals. His second week's objectives might look like this:

1. Each day at lunch I'll speak up by asking at least one question relating to what someone else is talking about.
2. During the conversation I'll express my opinion on at least one topic of discussion.

He decides to increase the number of questions from one to five and opinion statements from one to four. At lunch on Monday, Sam becomes too flustered after his first question to express an opinion. At home that evening, he realizes that his new goals are too high, that he's likely to give up in frustration if he doesn't adjust them. Accordingly, he modifies his goal to one question each day. By *gradually* increasing the amount of time he speaks up, Sam is able after several months to join in the conversations quite naturally and without thinking about the number of questions or statements he would try to make. You can see how the practice of planning questions eventually led him to feel much more natural around others.

I've used Sam's situation to lay out the rudiments of goal-setting. In the chapters geared to specific symptoms I give concrete suggestions for customizing this process to fit your own needs. Depending on your goal and situation, you can structure your steps differently. For instance, if you find that you can't sustain a conversation with a casual acquaintance for more than two minutes, your goal might be to increase the amount of time you keep the conversation going, gradually working up from two minutes to ten.

Remember to reward yourself for accomplishing your goal. If

there is an expensive item that you want to reward yourself with, you can use pennies or poker chips as intermediate rewards while you build up to your high-ticket item. Usually, the less time there is between achieving a goal and being rewarded, the better this system works. Therefore, you may find that to keep up your motivation you need to give yourself a small daily reward for accomplishing your goal. It could be something as simple as allowing yourself a half hour of uninterrupted time to read a book, listen to music, or take a walk. Experiment with rewards that you find pleasurable and with time intervals for giving yourself those rewards until you feel certain that you've set up a good system for yourself.

To summarize the process of successful goal-setting:

1. State your goals in specific terms.
2. If you don't succeed with a goal, break it down into small steps.
3. Reward yourself in proportion to your achievement.
4. Resist the temptation to try to change your behavior overnight.

You now have all the basic tools to begin your program to conquer your shyness. You've carefully answered the questionnaires, identified your specific symptoms, and drawn up a list of those situations in which you feel most nervous. Last of all, you've learned how to keep a self-development notebook and you have a good idea of how to set goals for yourself.

Thus far, I've pretty much asked you to play the role of observer of your shyness. In the next chapter you begin actively working on changing your behavior—by learning how to relax.

Relaxation Techniques for Overcoming Physical Symptoms

"SHYNESS CALLED HEREDITARY" . . . "DO YOU FEEL SHY? BLAME MOM AND DAD!" . . . "BORN TO BE SHY" . . . Those were just some of the headlines written about my research on the genetic aspect of shyness. They made me cringe! Nothing, to my mind, is more harmful than leading people to believe that they're helpless because of their own biological makeup. For a small percentage of the population genetics contributes to shyness. But should you give up the hope of changing yourself? Not at all. You may have inherited a tendency to shyness, and your upbringing and your experiences in life may have reinforced your tendency to be shy, but it's up to you to decide whether you'll remain a shrinking violet forever.

THE SHY TEMPERAMENT

We've all known someone who's a hothead—a person who loses his cool at the drop of a hat. If you talk to his parents, you'd probably find that even as an infant he had a temper. Shyness, like hotheadedness, can be an inherited temperament—an enduring biological predisposition to behave in certain ways.

Parents with two or more children know exactly what an inherited temperament is: almost from day one their children had distinctly different personalities. Some babies are colicky, fussy, and startle easily; others are guided effortlessly into a smooth routine of feeding, napping, and playing. Still others fear new surroundings and people, taking longer to adjust to changes in everything from their environment to new food or toys.[1] Current research suggests that about fifteen percent of Americans have an inherited tendency to be shy. This is the shy temperament.

If you are temperamentally shy, you know all too well how it expresses itself. There you are, involved in a new activity or with people you don't know well. Wham! Your heart begins to race, and though you may not know it, your pupils dilate, becoming wide with fear. Your body goes into stress-reaction overdrive. Your stomach turns somersaults; your mouth suddenly feels as though it's full of cotton just as you're about to speak; your palms become sweaty and your hands shake.

What's your first response? To back away from new people or strange surroundings, to blend in with the furniture. But don't feel like an oddball just because you have extreme physical reactions to new situations and people. Research with twins has demonstrated that we inherit our temperament.

Working with behavior geneticist Alan Zonderman, I used common scientific knowledge about twins in one of my studies to learn if shyness is an inherited trait.[2] I studied over eight hundred pairs of twins and found there is a genetic factor to shyness for some people. Filling out a questionnaire much like the one in Chapter 1, the identical and fraternal twins in my study showed differences in their degree of shyness. If one fraternal twin was shy, it didn't necessarily predict shyness in the other twin. But if one identical twin was shy, then the other twin tended to be just as shy. Since identical twins are genetically the same, I inferred that their shyness was partly inherited.

A number of other studies have also examined shyness in twins ranging in age from two months to fifty-five years of age.[3] These studies have shown that shyness may be the most inheritable of all personality traits; that this type of shyness begins during the first year of life (usually the latter half); and that unless steps are taken to overcome it, shyness is likely to endure as a lifelong personality trait.

NEW RESEARCH ON SHYNESS

One of my recent studies provides clues about the biological aspects of shyness. I was intrigued by Harvard psychologist Jerome Kagan's study of infants who had a high physical response to new people and situations, and by his finding that by the time these infants reached the age of five they were described by their own mothers and their kindergarten teachers as shy. What fascinated me was that Kagan also noticed that more often than not these shy children had blue eyes rather than brown.[4]

I decided to investigate the eye color difference in a group of several hundred white college students to see if their physical symptoms of shyness continued to show up in later life. It did. Students with blue eyes tended to have more physical symptoms of shyness than did the brown-eyed students.[5] Researchers now believe that the melanin that gives eyes their color is linked to the brain chemistry that controls the sensitivity of the nervous system. Blue eyes don't actually cause shyness, but they do seem to act as a "marker" for the tendency to have an overly sensitive nervous system. (Keep in mind that this research found that some brown-eyed people also have physical symptoms of shyness.)

While results of this study are preliminary, they're exciting because they provide evidence that our individual personality differences are somewhat grounded in our biological makeup. However, it's not nature versus nurture, but the interaction between them that will ultimately explain the development of our personalities and behavior.[6] Consider the example of height: Genes alone don't determine our height; our environment also has a strong influence. For example, since the end of World War II, better nutrition in Japan has increased the average height of Japanese men by about four inches.[7] An improved diet in Japan has allowed Japanese men's genes to realize their full potential.

LEARNING TO BE AFRAID

To see how nature interacts with nurture in personality development, we can look at a study by the famous behavioral psychologist John B. Watson.

In the 1920s, Watson conducted a series of experiments with a nine-month-old baby called "little Albert" that showed how our fears are learned.[8] Albert was a perfect subject for this experiment since in his short life he had had few encounters with either animals or reptiles, and thus had few impressions of them, either positive or negative.

Watson first placed Albert in a room and showed him a white rabbit. The baby's first reaction was curiosity—he reached out and touched the rabbit. Next, Watson had his assistant leave the room, taking the white rabbit with him, while Albert continued playing with his blocks. A short while later, Watson's assistant returned and again placed the rabbit near Albert, who eagerly approached his furry friend. But this time, just as Albert touched the rabbit, Watson himself, standing behind Albert, slammed a carpenter's hammer on a steel bar. The loud noise scared Albert, who began to cry, whimper, and look fearful.

Watson repeated the experiment twice more. When the white rabbit was brought to Albert for the third time, he cried out with fear at the sight of the small creature. Watson no longer needed to bang on the steel bar to frighten the child. Albert now associated the white rabbit with frightening noises. Even though it wasn't the rabbit that produced the fearful sounds, the white rabbit nevertheless became a feared object.

Watson continued his experiments and quickly discovered that other furry animals now frightened Albert as well. Albert even showed fear of a fur coat, a rug, and the fluffy white beard of a Santa Claus mask. His fearful response to the loud noise had become associated with all animals and objects resembling the rabbit, even though none of these animals or objects had previously been feared. It would be unethical to repeat this same experiment today, but you can see from it how our natural responses readily develop into fears.

TYING IT ALL TOGETHER

Many people, even those who don't think of themselves as shy, experience physical arousal in new situations. The difference lies in how they interpret that arousal. People who are not shy notice their arousal and simply attribute it to the circumstances. They don't let their racing heartbeat or nervousness stop them from doing what they want to do in the situation. For the shy person it's different. "Oh, no, here I go again," they say. *"Everyone* is going to see just how nervous I feel!" Shy people attribute their arousal to themselves, in a self-blaming way, rather than seeing the situation itself as the cause of arousal. The shy person is saying inwardly: "There's something wrong with me. I just have to get around new people or involved in a new activity and my whole body goes berserk. I'm hopeless."

You're not hopeless. Most likely your shy feelings were reinforced when you were young. Maybe you had outgoing parents who couldn't understand why you refused to join in the play group on your first day of nursery school. Not intending any harm, they may have pushed you too fast, expected you to be just as naturally outgoing as they were. The more you were pushed the more inadequate you felt. Or, perhaps your parents realized that you were shy and did their best to protect you from the social situations that made you uncomfortable. Inadvertently, by being overprotective, they denied you the opportunities to approach social activities at your own pace and in your own style. You might also have had older brothers and sisters or playmates who teased or bullied you, taking advantage of your "slow-to-warm-up" style, so instead of learning that once you adapted to a new situation there were pleasurable rewards—new things to do and new friends to be made—your shyness symptoms were reinforced. It became familiar to blush or shake or sweat. Just like little Albert, you learned to associate new people and new situations with physical discomfort.

As I said before, early-developing shyness—the genetic component of shyness—isn't predestined or inevitable. It's simply a *susceptibility* to shyness that develops when *reinforced* by experiences in life. Only about half of all shy adults have this inherited tendency to shyness; the other half develop their shyness later in life.

ARE YOU AN EARLY-DEVELOPING SHY PERSON?

Think about your most recent shyness experience. Sit down, close your eyes, and picture that event. I know it's painful, but let all those feelings sweep over you again. Now, as you're recalling the situation, how was your body responding? Read each of the descriptions below and circle the number that best describes your physical response to your shyness situations.

PHYSICAL SYMPTOMS OF SHYNESS

	NEVER	RARELY	SOMETIMES	OFTEN	ALWAYS
Sweating	0	1	2	3	4
Shaking/trembling	0	1	2	3	4
Pounding heart	0	1	2	3	4
Tense stomach ("butterflies")	0	1	2	3	4
Urge to urinate	0	1	2	3	4
Difficulty in breathing normally	0	1	2	3	4
Dry mouth	0	1	2	3	4
Blushing	0	1	2	3	4
Dizziness	0	1	2	3	4

Now add up your score. If you scored between 0 and 9, your problems aren't with the physical symptoms of shyness, but with anxious thoughts, worries, or awkward behaviors. If you scored between 10 and 17, then your physical symptoms are in the moderate range. You're an early-developing shy person. A score over 18 indicates that you're very physically sensitive in your shyness situations.

If you are an early-developing shy person, you now have a tremendous amount of power at your fingertips. That power is insight: you know you've got the shy temperament and now you can learn to master it, to control it instead of allowing it to control you.

Think you can't do it? Nonsense! You're not the only person who has to learn how to handle your temperament. Remember the hothead? What happens when the spitfire doesn't learn to control his temper? Jobs are lost, friendships broken, marriages destroyed. You just have a different kind of temperament, but you don't have to be victimized by it.

Many shy people tell me that they worry other people will notice their blushing or sweating or shaking. Here's the good news: Other people *don't* notice your physical symptoms as much as you think they do. Kimberley McEwan, of the University of Calgary, conducted a study to find out just how aware people are of the physical symptoms of shyness in others.[9] In her investigation, she had shy people list their physical symptoms and rate how noticeable they felt their symptoms to be to others. She then had a friend of each shy participant indicate how much he or she noticed physical arousal in that person. The results of her study showed that those with high levels of physical arousal believed that they displayed a greater number of visible signs of shyness than were actually noticed by their friends. So, as you confront your shy situations, remember that your symptoms of shyness aren't nearly as visible to others as you might believe.

A word about medications: There are anti-anxiety drugs that help people who experience severe panic attacks. Originally developed for high blood pressure, these drugs work by keeping your heart rate steady. If you have acute panic attacks, ask your doctor about these drugs. For most people, though, drugs *aren't* necessary. You can learn to reduce anxiety naturally without falling prey to the dependency and side effects of drugs.[10]

HOW TO STAY CALM IN A SOCIAL SITUATION

A proven method for combating anxiety is a technique called *systematic desensitization,* which helps replace your physical arousal with a feeling of relaxation.[11]

There are three key steps to systematic desensitization:

1. Learn a relaxation method.
2. Build a hierarchy of an uncomfortable situation.
3. Use mental imagery to visualize each step in your hierarchy while remaining deeply relaxed.

You must first practice a relaxation technique at least once a day for two weeks before you incorporate your visualizations into it. The next step is to build your hierarchy of an uncomfortable situation. If you like, you can work on this while you're learning to relax. In the third step, you'll begin mental visualization after you've gotten yourself very relaxed with one of the two relaxation methods described below.

The key to making this technique work is mental imagery, which many of us are familiar with.

MENTAL IMAGERY   Most of us daydream from time to time, and daydreaming is really just mental imagery. We each have a mental screen on which we see images of people, objects, and situations. Often emotions accompany our mental images. The more strongly you can see and feel yourself in an imagined situation, the more effective visualization will be for you when practicing systematic desensitization.

Does mental imagery work? To find out how mental imagery works, Sydney Segal and Vincent Fusella repeated an experiment on mental imagery that had first been done in 1910. Segal and Fusella asked some of the participants in their experiment to form a visual image in their minds and asked others to imagine a sound. A faint dot on a screen was shown to those visualizing a scene, while those imagining a sound wore headphones over which a faint sound was transmitted. In both groups the visualization process interfered with their ability to see the dot or hear the sound. The two researchers concluded that the images we form in our minds resemble actual perceptions of sight and sound. Why this is so is uncertain; it may be because the parts of the brain that we use for imagining are the same areas used for actual sight and sound perceptions.

In another experiment, Alan Richardson asked participants without prior experience in gymnastics to mentally rehearse for six days a simple exercise on the horizontal bar. During the five-minute mental rehearsal each day, participants were encouraged to "see and feel themselves" go through the exercise. After their sixth day of mental rehearsal, participants were asked to actually perform the exercise on the horizontal bar and their routine was scored. Richardson found that people with vivid and controllable imagery performed much better than those with weak imaginations.[12]

What does this have to do with your shyness problem? It means you can use your imagination to rehearse your shy situations, visualizing yourself calm and relaxed. When you can do this you'll be able to confront uncomfortable situations knowing that you'll remain unflustered through it all.

Julie's example shows how mental imagery works. Julie, twenty-nine, is a corporate lawyer working for a small firm in New York City. She seems headed for success, putting in long hours and doing excellent work. Her only stumbling block is her paralyzing shyness during staff meetings. Each time she's called upon to speak, Julie's face flushes, her stomach tightens into knots, and her hands shake violently.

Through systematic desensitization Julie has taken control of her physical symptoms of shyness. Here's how she did it.

Julie started her program by first learning how to relax. She chose the progressive relaxation technique and practiced it twice each day for two weeks. She set her alarm clock to awaken her twenty minutes earlier than usual and went through her relaxation exercise before breakfast. When she returned home in the evenings, she again practiced relaxation before sitting down for dinner. At the end of each day she marked down in her self-development notebook how many times she practiced relaxing and how she felt she was doing.

While she was learning to relax, Julie also worked on the hierarchy for her situation: blushing, shaking, and a tense stomach when she's the focus of attention during staff meetings. The steps in her hierarchy were these:

1. Thinking about the weekly staff meeting.
2. Thinking about the weekly staff meeting the day before it's scheduled.
3. Waking up the morning of the staff meeting.
4. Riding the subway to work the day of the staff meeting.
5. Preparing notes for the staff meeting.
6. Walking into the conference room and sitting down.
7. Chatting with coworkers while waiting for everyone to assemble.
8. Listening to the senior partner bring the meeting to order, and his summary of important company business.
9. Hearing the request for her report on the status of one of her cases.
10. Giving her report on her case.

Julie wrote out vignettes—short descriptions—of each step in her hierarchy. Then she set out her goals for practicing systematic desensitization:

1. I'll practice systematic desensitization for thirty minutes five times a week.
2. I'll begin systematic desensitization on July 30th and continue until I have visualized all the vignettes while remaining very relaxed.
3. After I've worked through the last vignette, I'll go to the next staff meeting knowing that I'll remain calm and relaxed when I'm called on.

Julie kept careful track of her progress with relaxation, and beginning on July 30th carefully noted in her self-development notebook each day that she completed a session of systematic desensitization. Each session she pictured herself with her face its normal color, her body posture confident, and her stomach calm and relaxed. By the time she'd worked through all of her vignettes, Julie was able to enter staff meetings calmly and confidently. As time passed, it became easier and easier for her to participate in the regular staff meetings knowing that she wouldn't be blushing or shaking or sending her stomach into knots. To celebrate her success, Julie treated herself to a Broadway show that she'd been longing to see. Encouraged by her achievement, Julie's next goal is to tackle her shy situation of conferring with lawyers outside her firm.

RELAXATION METHODS

The first step in systematic desensitization is to learn and practice a relaxation method. To give instructions on the many methods of relaxation would require a book in itself, so from the list below I'll provide detailed instructions for two of them: progressive relaxation and a variation of TM. I suggest you try both methods and then choose the one that works best for you. If you find that neither of the methods described works for you, you may want to investigate classes in one of the other methods noted below.[13]

- *Autogenic Training:* Developed by Dr. H. H. Shultz, a German neurologist, autogenic training consists of six mental exercises to bring on relaxation. The mental attitude during autogenic training is often compared to self-hypnosis.
- *Progressive Relaxation:* Created by Dr. Edward Jacobsen, this technique uses a procedure of tensing and then relaxing muscles.
- *Self-Hypnosis:* Hypnosis that is self-induced is referred to as self-hypnosis. In the hypnotic trance, you filter out external perceptions and focus on internal perceptions. You can use self-hypnosis for relaxation by giving yourself suggestions for a relaxed mind and body.
- *Transcendental Meditation (TM):* Brought to the West by Maharishi Mahesh Yogi, TM is practiced for twenty minutes twice a day. Deep relax-

ation is brought on by repeating a mantra; the mantra decreases mental activity, enabling the meditator to reach a higher state of consciousness.

- *Yoga:* A school of Indian philosophy, yoga emphasizes the regulation of breathing and the adoption of specified body postures (for example, the lotus position).

For either of the relaxation methods detailed below, you should follow these conditions:

1. Find a quiet place where you can relax undisturbed. Unplug the phone; if others are in the house with you, ask that they don't disturb you.
2. Choose a comfortable chair to sit in. It's better not to lie down—you may relax so completely that you fall asleep!
3. Don't practice relaxation within two hours after a meal. The digestion process will interfere with your ability to relax.
4. Practice your relaxation method at least once a day, but not more than twice a day.
5. Give yourself time! The reason that I recommend practicing a relaxation method for two weeks before incorporating mental visualizations into it is because it takes at least that long for most people to learn to relax completely. On the surface it might seem that relaxing is easy to do, but for many of us it isn't. Try not to become frustrated with your first few attempts at relaxation—it takes a while to become proficient at it.

Progressive Relaxation

The easiest way to learn this technique is to tape-record the instructions so that you don't have to keep looking in a book to follow along; it will help you experience relaxation more completely and with greater ease. When you make your recording, keep your voice as soothing and as evenly paced as you can; try to speak in a monotone. You'll notice at the end of the exercise that you'll be saying the word "relax" to yourself with each breath out. Later you can use this as a cue when you suddenly find yourself tensing up in a social situation. Take a deep breath, and as you exhale, say to yourself "relax" and try to recall the total feeling of relaxation you experience during your practice.

A note of caution about progressive relaxation: When you're tensing your muscles, don't go overboard—you only want to feel the difference between moderate muscle tension and relaxation.

Instructions: Sit comfortably with your arms loosely at your side, your feet and hands placed comfortably, but not crossed. Close your eyes and breathe in and out through your nose. Instructions in parentheses indicate times to let the tape recorder continue running before you speak again.

Squeeze your right hand into a fist (pause for 5 seconds). Now slowly relax your hand and feel the difference between the tension and the relaxation. Again, squeeze your right hand into a fist (pause for 5 seconds). Slowly relax your hand and feel the difference. Continue to breathe in and out through your nose.

Now squeeze your left hand into a fist (pause for 5 seconds). Slowly relax your hand and feel the difference between the tension and the relaxation. Again, squeeze your left hand into a fist (pause for 5 seconds). Slowly relax your hand and feel the difference. Notice how relaxed both hands now feel.

Now bend your right elbow, making your right hand into a fist and tensing your forearm and upper arm (pause for 5 seconds). Straighten your arm and let your fist and arm relax. Continue breathing through your nose. Once again, bend your right elbow, making your right hand into a fist and tensing your forearm and upper arm (pause for 5 seconds). Next, straighten your arm and let your fist and arm completely relax. Enjoy the warm feeling of total relaxation in the muscles of your hand and arm.

Bend your left elbow, making your left hand into a fist and tensing your forearm and upper arm (pause for 5 seconds). Straighten your arm and let your fist and arm relax. Notice the difference between tension and relaxation. Once again, bend your left elbow, making your left hand into a fist and tensing your forearm and upper arm (pause for 5 seconds). Now straighten your arm and slowly relax your fist and arm. Take a moment to enjoy how relaxed your arms and hands are (pause for 5 seconds).

Next, move your head in a circular motion, twice to the left and twice to the right. Turn your head to the right as far as you can (pause for five seconds). And now face forward again and feel how wonderfully relaxed your neck is becoming. Again, turn your head to the right as far as you can (pause for 5 seconds). Now slowly relax and face forward again. Continue to breathe through your nose.

Turn your head to the left as far as you can (pause for 5 seconds). Face forward and again, turn your head to the left as far as you can (pause for 5 seconds). Now face forward again. Bend your head forward and press your chin against your chest (pause for 5 seconds). Lift your head up and enjoy the peaceful feeling of relaxation in your neck, arms, and hands.

Now turn your attention to your shoulders. Shrug your shoulders, bringing them up as high as you can (pause for 5 seconds). Release the tension in your shoulders, allowing them to sink slowly back down. Continue to breathe through your nose. Once again, shrug your shoulders, bringing them up as high as you can (pause for 5 seconds). Then release the tension, letting your shoulders fall back down gently. Notice the difference between tension and relaxation.

Now arch your eyebrows as high as you can (pause for 5 seconds). Release. Again arch your eyebrows, bringing them up toward the top of your head (pause for 5 seconds). And now release, feeling your forehead relax. Next, squint your eyes (pause for 5 seconds), then relax. Again, squint your eyes (pause for 5 seconds) and release, feeling the tension flow away from your eyes. Continue to breathe through your nose. Purse your lips tightly together (pause for 5 seconds). Slowly relax your lips. Once more, purse your lips tightly together (pause for 5 seconds), then relax. Immerse yourself in the feeling of relaxation: your arms and hands . . . your shoulders and neck . . . your face . . . all are deeply relaxed. Enjoy that feeling of deep relaxation.

Now tense the muscles in your upper back: raise your shoulders up and push them back as far as you can (pause for 5 seconds). Let your shoulders drop, concentrating on the relaxed feeling in your back. Again, raise your shoulders up, push them back as far as you can (pause for 5 seconds), then let them drop. Notice the difference between tension and relaxation.

And now as you are relaxing more and more, breathe in deeply. Fill your lungs as full as you can and hold your breath (pause for 5 seconds). Slowly release the air and breathe normally for a few moments. Feel the waves of relaxation wash over you; enjoy the peaceful feeling of being totally relaxed. Once again, breathe in deeply, filling your lungs as full as you can and holding your breath (pause for 5 seconds). Slowly release the air and now breathe normally through your nose (pause for 10 seconds). Again, breathe in deeply. Fill your lungs as full as you can and hold your breath (pause for 5 seconds). Slowly release the air. Breathe in and out normally through your nose and feel the sensations of being rested and relaxed.

Next, move your attention to the muscles in your stomach. Tighten your stomach and abdominal muscles (pause for 5 seconds). Then slowly release the tension, noticing how good it feels to relax the muscles. Once more, tighten your stomach and abdominal muscles (pause for 5 seconds) and release. Continue to breathe through your nose. Feel the deep relaxation in your arms and hands, your neck and shoulders, your face, your back, and stomach.

Now arch your back and tighten the muscles (pause for 5 seconds). Release, noticing the difference between tension and relaxation. Arch your back again and tighten the muscles (pause for 5 seconds). And now relax, feeling the tension drain away from your lower back.

Now tighten the muscles in your buttocks, thighs, hips, legs, and calves. Tense the muscles in your buttocks and press down on the heels of your feet (pause for 5 seconds). Release the tension and slowly relax. Again, tense the muscles in your buttocks and press down on the heels of your feet (pause for 5 seconds). Release the tension, continue to breathe through your nose, and feel how heavy and relaxed your lower body feels.

Next, point your toes toward your head and tighten all of the muscles in your feet, ankles, and lower legs (pause for 5 seconds).

Release. Again, point your toes toward your head and tighten all of the muscles in your feet, ankles, and lower legs (pause for 5 seconds). Then slowly relax these muscles, noticing the difference between tension and relaxation.

Now you are so very relaxed. All of your muscles feel heavy. You're enjoying the sensations of complete and total relaxation. Breathe slowly and deeply as you continue to feel completely relaxed. With each breath out, say to yourself "relax" (or "calm" or "let go"). Continue breathing in and out through your nose slowly and deeply, repeating the word "relax" with each breath out (pause for 60 seconds). Feel the gentle waves of relaxation wash over you. Enjoy the serenity of being completely relaxed. Savor all of these feelings for several minutes more.

A Variation of TM

Another method of relaxation, based on Transcendental Meditation, is one developed by Dr. Herbert Benson.[14] To practice his technique you'll need to set aside ten to twenty minutes twice each day. Some people find it easiest to practice this method just before breakfast and again just before dinner time.

Instructions:

1. Sit in a comfortable position.
2. Close your eyes.
3. Relax all of your muscles, beginning at your feet and continuing up to your face.
4. Adopt a passive attitude. Disregard any distracting thoughts and try to maintain a "let it happen" attitude.
5. Breathe through your nose. As you breathe out, say the word "one" silently to yourself. By repeating the word "one" each time you exhale, you help reduce distracting thoughts that may enter your mind.
6. Continue repeating the word "one" with each breath out for ten to twenty minutes.
7. Don't use an alarm clock to tell you when the time is up! Instead, open your eyes occasionally to check the time. Remain sitting quietly for a few minutes after you've finished.

BUILDING YOUR HIERARCHIES

While you're learning a relaxation method, you can begin building a hierarchy of one of your shyness situations from the last exercise in Chapter 1. I recommend that you begin with the situation on your list that is *least* uncomfortable, gradually working your way up to the one that's *most* uncomfortable.

To begin you'll need a stack of 3 × 5 index cards. On each card you'll be writing a short descriptive scene of each aspect of your situation that brings on your physical symptoms. There are three different types of hierarchies you can choose from to write your descriptions.

The first type is a distance hierarchy, in which you describe and rank the aspects of your problem in terms of the distance in space or time from your uncomfortable situation. For example, you want to ask your coworker, Darcy, to have lunch with you. Using a distance hierarchy with physical space as the criterion, your cards might look like this:

Leaving your house to go to work	*Walking down the hall to Darcy's office*
Entering your office building	*Walking into Darcy's office*
Entering your office	*Standing opposite Darcy and asking her to have lunch with you*

The same situation with time as the criterion of your hierarchy could run like this:

On Saturday morning, thinking about asking Darcy to have lunch with you on Monday		*Arriving in your office and setting yourself up for the day's work*
On Sunday evening, rehearsing your lunch invitation to Darcy		*At 10 A.M. walking down the hallway to Darcy's office*
Driving to work on Monday morning, rehearsing your invitation again		*Asking Darcy if she's free to have lunch with you today*

A second type of hierarchy is theme-oriented. In this type of arrangement, hierarchies vary in each aspect with the theme. For example, suppose one of your shyness situations is meeting new people. You can write out the descriptions in terms of meeting one new person, all the way up to being introduced to ten new people at once. For example:

Being introduced to a new person by someone I already know		*Introducing myself to two new people*
Introducing myself to a new person		*Being introduced to four new people by someone I know*
Being introduced to two new people by someone I already know		*Introducing myself to four new people*

The last type of hierarchy is mixed, combining both the elements of theme and space/time. I believe that mixed hierarchies may be the most useful because they provide a more realistic approach to gradually building up to your uncomfortable situation. To return to the example used above, suppose you're scheduled to attend a seminar where there will be people you already know as well as unfamiliar people. Your mixed hierarchy could be written out like this:

Thinking about meeting new people at the seminar tomorrow

Chatting with a coworker and glancing around the seminar room

Driving to the seminar where there will be new people to meet

Walking over to the coffee urn with my coworker, where he introduces me to someone new

Walking into the seminar room and greeting someone I already know

Introducing myself to a new person at the lunch break

Think about the situation you're going to tackle first, and decide which type of hierarchy you think will work best for you. Begin writing one short descriptive scene on each index card. As you write, you'll probably find that you'll need to add a few more steps and descriptions. Most hierarchies consist of between ten and thirty descriptions, depending on the situation. Just be sure that your descriptions don't jump from one that causes you only mild discomfort to one that causes you a great deal of discomfort. It's important that each description build up slowly to the last card.

Once you've written out the descriptions of each aspect of your shyness situation, double-check to be sure your cards are in order from least uncomfortable to most uncomfortable. When you feel proficient with your relaxation method, you're ready to set your goals and begin combining relaxation with visualization.

SET YOUR GOALS

Before you begin combining relaxation with visualization, you'll need to set your goals. Remember: your goals should be attainable and specific. You might want to begin by writing out this goal: "I will practice my relaxation method twice a day from April 3rd through April 17th." Write down the dates in your self-development notebook and note after each date the number of times you practiced your relaxation method.

Next you'll need to set goals for practicing systematic desensitization. Your goal could be to practice for a specified number of minutes each day or for a specified number of minutes at least four times a week until you have successfully worked through one shyness situation. As you work up through the rankings of your shy situations, keep writing out and tracking your goals for each one.

Finally, remember to give yourself a nice reward for accomplishing your goal!

Relax and Visualize

When you feel ready to begin combining relaxation with visualization, choose a block of time when you can commit at least several days during the week to practicing it. As you did during your relaxation sessions, be certain that you're in a comfortable place where you won't be disturbed. An easy way to combine relaxation with visualization is to tape-record your descriptions. If you choose to use a tape recorder, speak slowly and clearly into the recorder and allow the tape to run for a few minutes before you read your next card. You can also simply read each card to yourself if you don't have ready access to a tape recorder.

Once you're deeply relaxed, turn on your tape recorder or read each card to yourself and visualize yourself as you've described the scene on each card. While remaining very relaxed, hear or read your first description. See and feel yourself in that situation while remaining relaxed. When you can picture yourself in your first description and remain relaxed, continue to the next one. Again, picture yourself in the description and remain relaxed. As soon as you get to a description where you can't stay relaxed, stop the visualization, relax yourself completely again, and try the description once more. Repeat this process until you can work through the difficult scene while remaining relaxed. Then proceed to the next description.

You may find that you can get through the first few descriptions quite easily and then get stuck on the third or fourth one. Be patient with yourself and keep working with it until you succeed. The more vividly you can imagine yourself in the scene, the more effectively systematic desensitization will work for you. Imagine yourself feeling and behaving socially poised in each description—picture and feel yourself this way. Once you've successfully visualized yourself in your first shyness situation, try it out in the real world. When you're satisfied that the process is working for you, you'll be ready to build a new hierarchy for the next situation in your shyness list. It's certainly a process that requires time, but it works. Give yourself plenty of time and patience to work through all the descriptions at your own pace.

IF YOU ARE HAVING PROBLEMS REACHING YOUR GOALS . . .

Sometimes you'll find that you're having great difficulty accomplishing your goals. The first question to ask yourself is: Are my goals reasonably attainable? Perhaps you've decided to practice systematic desensitization every day, but your life is really quite busy. Go easier on yourself and reduce the number of days each week that you'll practice. Keep your goals within the realm of the possible in terms of available time and your energy level.

A second question to ask yourself is: Do I need to break my goals down further? Perhaps weeks on end seems hopeless to you, something you just can't imagine sticking to. If that is the case, change your goal to one that you set week by week. At the end of each week, when you've successfully completed your goal, give yourself a small reward. Then set up your goal again for the next week.

Whenever you find yourself having undue difficulties, play Twenty Questions with yourself until you discover the source of your stumbling block. Usually, if you examine carefully what it is about the circumstances that is causing you delays, you can figure out a way to surmount the problem.

Even after you've struggled to identify your stumbling blocks in a particular circumstance, you may still find yourself thinking,

"This is too hard . . . I wouldn't know what to say in this situation . . . Deep down I don't like myself enough to believe that others would like me . . . I can't imagine ever handling this situation successfully . . ."

When you find yourself despairing, it's time for you to *temporarily* stop your relaxing and visualizing program. Work on the exercises in Chapters 3 through 5. Begin building up your self-esteem, learn to stop negative thoughts, and brush up on your social skills. Then come back to your relaxing and visualizing program. You'll find it easier to imagine yourself in a situation when you're feeling better about yourself, when you're thinking positively, and when you know what social skills to apply to a situation. Work back and forth through the chapters, combining techniques for maximum effectiveness.

To summarize: Systematic desensitization is an excellent device for overcoming the physical symptoms of shyness. You can use the technique over and over again throughout your life. Even if you find yourself backsliding, you can return to your goals and visualize your way through them again. You can also use the process to help yourself work through similar difficulties you may be having in other areas of your life.

I hope that you'll want to continue practicing your relaxation method even when you're finished with systematic desensitization. Relaxation has many benefits to offer—increased energy and mental alertness, lower blood pressure, and better sleeping patterns.

Even after you've made progress by applying the relaxation techniques in this chapter, the physical symptoms of shyness may occasionally be a problem for you. After all, what you've learned to do in this chapter is merely to recondition a *natural* response of your body. Nevertheless, whenever you find yourself responding to a new situation or person with physical symptoms, use them as a signal. Say to yourself, "Oh, my heart is starting to pound—that's a signal for me to take a few deep breaths and concentrate on relaxing myself for a moment." Remember that most people aren't even noticing the physical arousal that seems so apparent to you. The best thing, though, is that as you continue on your social path, despite feeling shy inside, you'll help create a positive cycle of reinforcement for yourself.

CHAPTER 3

Building Self-Esteem

Shy people are notorious for giving themselves a mental kick in the pants each time they behave shyly. Each time they fade into the background, keep their thoughts to themselves, or pass up an opportunity to meet new people they take themselves down a notch. Chances are you feel like Jillian, a forty-one-year-old business manager: "I often wish I could free myself from my feelings of low self-esteem and self-consciousness. It's a constant struggle between really wanting to be noticed and at the same time a desperate fear of being noticed."

Low self-esteem and self-consciousness are the two hallmarks of late-developing shyness, which begins between the ages of ten and fourteen. For many teenagers shyness is often no more than a temporarily awkward phase of growing up. For others, however, shyness persists into adulthood, bringing with it crippling pessimism and perpetual low self-esteem.[1] Even early-developing shy persons are likely to find that the challenges of adolescence intensify their shy feelings. For them, the difficulties of forming a self-assured adult identity are compounded by the physical distress they already experience.

In the next few pages I want to show you how your shyness connects with the value you place on yourself and suggest some methods for increasing your self-esteem. (We'll go into self-consciousness in the next chapter.)

DO YOU HAVE LOW SELF-ESTEEM?

During the fall of my senior year at George Washington University, I was busy preparing applications to graduate school. One afternoon I buttonholed my favorite professor in the corridor and asked him to write a letter of recommendation for me. He gladly agreed, accepting the typewritten list of schools to which I was applying. His eyes scanned the page and then his smile turned into a frown. "Jonathan, these schools are okay, but where's Princeton, where's Harvard?"

I stammered out something about being sure of acceptance.

He shoved the list back at me. "You're selling yourself short."

Selling yourself short is just one symptom of low self-esteem. Rejecting yourself, anticipating rejection from others, judging yourself harshly, avoiding risks (and hence possible failure), and being a perfectionist are other ways low self-esteem expresses itself. I was fortunate that my path crossed with that of someone who cared. If it weren't for my professor encouraging me to recognize my potential I might not have fulfilled my academic and career aspirations.

Changing how you feel about yourself is a tough business, like reversing the direction of a fast-spinning merry-go-round. People who undervalue themselves typically react to situations with negative thoughts and feelings. Those around them quickly learn that they don't treat themselves well and, hence, in turn, may not extend them the respect and consideration they deserve. This reinforces the person's innate feelings of worthlessness— "I must deserve this, otherwise why would anyone treat me this way?"—and the cycle is perpetuated.

Think for a moment: Are you essentially happy with yourself? Can you honestly say, "I like who I am"? A negative answer doesn't mean you necessarily walk around consciously consumed with self-loathing. (Fortunately, few of us are so consumed with alienation that we think of ourselves in the same terms as Kafka's Gregor Samsa, who woke up one morning to find himself transformed into a giant dung beetle.) Low self-esteem operates more subtly than that. Below is a list of adjectives that pinpoints a range of negative attitudes. Think about yourself and carefully consider the list of feelings, checking off the ones that you'd use to describe yourself. (The list will prove helpful when you begin changing the way you think about yourself.)

Low Self-Esteem Feelings

I feel:

☐ inept	☐ useless
☐ unlovable	☐ insecure
☐ insignificant	☐ inferior
☐ unwanted	☐ unloved
☐ self-rejecting	☐ self-contempt
☐ dissatisfied	☐ inadequate
☐ unassertive	☐ withdrawn
☐ weak	☐ frustrated

HIGH SELF-ESTEEM

The essence of high self-esteem is accepting and liking yourself. When you have high self-esteem you respect yourself as well as those around you; you feel certain in the core of yourself that you're a worthy person. Now, notice that I didn't say a *perfect* person, I said a *worthy* person. High self-esteem doesn't demand perfection, but expects room for growth and improvement. Possessing high self-esteem is being kind to yourself, confident that you're lovable, likable, competent, effective. You move through daily life assured of yourself. High self-esteem creates a positive cycle: When you feel good about yourself other people sense it in the way you treat both yourself and them; they respond favorably to you and their response reinforces your positive feelings about yourself.[2]

Consider what's special about you, what's unique about you, what your values are. Think about all the aspects of yourself that you like. Then, in the list below check off the adjectives that you'd use to describe yourself.

HIGH SELF-ESTEEM FEELINGS

I feel:

☐ self-assured	☐ valuable
☐ confident	☐ self-respecting
☐ worthy	☐ content
☐ relaxed	☐ capable
☐ adequate	☐ lovable
☐ likable	☐ effective
☐ significant	☐ loved
☐ secure	☐ self-accepting

How many adjectives did you check off? Compare the total with that of the previous list. Do you have more high self-esteem feelings or more low self-esteem feelings? Wouldn't you like to have the balance tilted more toward the positive end?

THE SOURCES OF SELF-ESTEEM

Beginning with our earliest days as children, life bombards us with experiences from which we piece together "good" or "bad" impressions of ourselves.[3] When we get lots of warm attention and plenty of hugs, we interpret that as positive information. We must be good because we're getting good things. But when someone yells at us that we're "stupid" or "lazy," we perceive that as criticism and wonder what's wrong with us.

In our very early years, parents wield the greatest influence on how we feel about ourselves. We know, for example, that parents with high self-esteem tend to raise children who also value themselves highly, just as parents with a low sense of self-worth are likely to rear children in their own image, unable to love themselves. Parents who ignore their children altogether do the most to undermine their children's healthy self-regard. Sadly, even an openly disapproving parent does more for a child's self-esteem than an indifferent father or mother; expressions of displeasure at least show children that they matter. Constant criticism and punishment won't do much to build high self-esteem, but a total lack of discipline tells children they aren't worth a parent's time or effort.

As we grow older and enter school, teachers (and other authorities) play increasingly larger roles in our self-concept. The classroom becomes another important building ground for self-esteem —and shyness. When we do well in school, we feel good about ourselves and our abilities. We feel competent and able. (For some children, however, earlier family experiences make it hard for them to accept their own successes.) When we get a failing grade, we may feel inadequate or stupid and stop trying. The kind of reinforcement we get in school makes a difference too. A parent or teacher who encourages improvement and rewards effort will help a youngster onto the path of high self-esteem. Consistent demands for perfection only erode our sense of self-worth.

The acid test of self-esteem arrives with adolescence. All of a sudden our bodies begin the metamorphosis into adult form—it is exciting, longed for, and frightening. As our bodies undergo change we encounter new opportunities for entering the adult world, yet in many ways, not all of them pleasant, we remain children. Parents and teachers may be reluctant to treat us as maturing individuals. It seems that everyone is now watching and judging us.

The uncertainty of adolescence can create feelings of shyness for the first time or build on feelings of shyness already in us. High school can be extraordinarily rough—it seems to be the first time when acceptance from our peers means *everything,* as reported by two shy people from one of my studies.

"When I was in high school," said Monica, "I had a really hard time making friends in the cliques. When I tried to talk to people I'd get very nervous because I was afraid they'd think I wasn't good enough for them."

Shelby recalled, "I became conscious of my shyness in high school. I didn't have many friends and spent most of my time alone. I had trouble talking with people comfortably because I was always nervous. I was aware of feelings of self-consciousness and low self-esteem. I still experience those feelings now."

Why does it seem that everyone else emerged from adolescence as confident young adults while you still feel as painfully shy and self-conscious as when you entered adolescence? There may have been significant life events that amplified your shy feelings.

SIGNIFICANT SHYNESS EVENTS

In a 1985 study, F. Ishu Ishiyama explored the roots of people's shyness. He concentrated on three factors: specific events that people remembered as contributing to their shyness; "non-incidental" causes (general life circumstances); and family structure.[4] A whopping seventy-two percent of his participants could name specific events that fostered their shyness, a figure whose accuracy I've confirmed in my own work. For example, Kari, a shy student in one of my studies, explains how her life changed when her family broke apart: "After fourth grade, my parents divorced and I was no longer able to attend the private school I'd gone to for first through fourth grade. All of my friends from that school went on to another private school; I had to attend public school and I felt like an outsider. Then I went to another school for junior high and again I felt like an outsider and very shy. This feeling has remained to the present day."

Changing schools or moving to a new neighborhood between

the ages of eight and fourteen is particularly stressful. Just as you become comfortable with people and places, you're abruptly thrust into a whole new world. Shaky self-confidence doesn't help as you enter a neighborhood or school where it seems that everyone's known each other since kindergarten.

Sometimes shyness is shaped by your relationships with important adults in your life. A coworker of mine recently told me about a high-school English teacher who absolutely intimidated her. One day in class Anna volunteered an answer to her teacher's question about the book the class was reading. Giving what she thought was the correct response, Anna was dumbfounded when her teacher said, "How could you be so stupid to think that?" Feeling embarrassed and foolish, Anna wisely kept all further comments and questions to herself. At the end of the year, her teacher had the audacity to write on her report card "Anna doesn't participate in class"! It took years for Anna to recover from this blow to her self-esteem and even as a returning student to college in her mid-forties she was still reluctant to speak up in class.

Wittingly or unwittingly, our parents' responses to us can promote shyness. As one of my research participants admits: "I didn't have a happy childhood or relationship with my mother. I feel I wasn't accepted as myself, so rather than become as my parent expected, I retreated into myself." Others may have been sheltered, like Frances, another participant in my research study: "As an only child, I was very protected and sheltered by my parents, and as a consequence, regarded anything or anyone new with fright and suspicion." Perhaps the adults around you labeled you as shy, as this forty-five-year-old businessman relates: "My parents and teachers defined me as shy; I think their definitions reinforced my shyness. I feel that a little praise and encouragement from my parents when I was young probably would've helped me to be a little less shy and more confident."

Shyness also springs from teasing and ridicule. Girls and boys who mature early or late, relative to their peers, come in for special negative recognition. As if all these conditions weren't enough, Ishiyama found that punishment, rejection, or criticism for shy behavior, and even punishment for being too talkative, intensified people's shy feelings.

We can't leave this long list of "things gone wrong" in our earliest years without mentioning the two predicaments that still send every shy adult running for the door: being forced to socialize and being the focus of attention.

YOUR SIGNIFICANT SHYNESS EVENTS

Were there specific events in your life that contributed to your shyness? If you were participating in one of my studies, what could you tell me about them? Try to recall events from your childhood or early adolescence that seemed to cement your shy feelings and jot them down in the space below or in your self-development notebook.

The non-incidental factors in Ishiyama's study weren't recalled as specifically painful, but their corrosive effects could still be seen over time. Some of Ishiyama's participants, for example, who weren't encouraged to get out and make friends or who had limited opportunities for meeting new people considered these circumstances important causes of their shyness. Worries about physical appearance and anticipation of rejection or humiliation were also frequently mentioned by his participants as shyness-inducing.

The third major factor Ishiyama uncovered was the shy person's family structure. Being an only child or, on the other hand, being caught up in a sibling rivalry with constant ridicule aggravated shyness. A few of his participants felt that having shy parents contributed to their own timidity.

What were your "non-incidental" causes of shyness? Were you encouraged to be outgoing? In what ways were your feelings of shyness reinforced? What was your family structure? Were you an only child, the oldest child, the middle child, or the youngest child? Did you have an older or younger brother or sister who got all the attention? Think of all the general life circumstances that may have contributed to your shyness and write them down below in the space or in your self-development notebook.

I know it can be painful reliving past events, but examining the sources of your shyness can help you understand how you got the way you are today. Research shows that many shy people subscribe to the irrational belief that the influence of the past can't be overcome. Instead of allowing your past to keep a firm grip on your present life, understand how you learned to be shy—but don't wallow in the past! The healthy step is to recognize the sources of your shyness, forgive the people who let you down in the past, and use your new insight to take charge of your life in a way you couldn't as a child. As a therapist friend of mine says about these things, "You came by it honestly." You did the best you could to cope as a youngster. That was then. This is now—and your life is under your control.

BODY ESTEEM

Closely connected to how we feel about our inner self is how we feel about our outer self—our physical body. It's tempting to believe that attractive people have it made. After all, aren't they always confident and assured, never socially maladroit? Well, no. If you don't feel good about your inner self, it doesn't much matter whether you're a beauty or not. Even people whom we'd define as all-American pretty or handsome suffer from shyness, like thirty-three-year-old Fiona: "I've always been shy. It doesn't have anything to do with my looks; I'm very attractive and intelligent, so I don't know why I seem to feel inadequate sometimes."

Many shy people judge themselves as unattractive. My colleague Wendy Liebman and I conducted a study among college women and found that the shy women consistently rated themselves as very physically unattractive.[5] Yet college men who hadn't met these women judged them by their photographs to be almost as attractive as socially self-confident women whose photos they were also shown. The shy women in our study were unrealistically critical of their physical appearance. They extended their inner feelings of self-doubt to include their outer appearance—despite what their mirrors might have told them.

I've also found that this irrational negative self-appraisal includes self-judgments of academic ability.[6] When shy and non-shy students were asked to rate their academic ability, the shy students invariably labeled themselves less competent than the socially confident students, but the two groups had identical grade point averages!

You might dream of weighing a little less or a little more, of changing the shape of your nose, or adding inches to your height in the belief that your shyness would then magically disappear overnight. Admittedly, it's hard for any of us to be satisfied with our bodies when TV, movies, and books present us with only supersleek images. However, just ask someone whom you consider to have a "perfect" body if he or she has any complaints, and you'll probably hear a string of them. Accepting our outer selves with a realistic and accurate evaluation is just as important as accepting and loving our inner selves. Outer changes can help, but they can't completely solve your inner self-doubts.

BODY-ESTEEM EXERCISE

Your mind and body work together, constantly interacting. Try to notice your posture the next time you're around other people. Are you slouching, staring at your feet? Do you feel awkward? Is your body reflecting your inner turmoil? If so, there are several things you can do to improve your body image.

Practice this technique in front of a full-length mirror: Stand undressed in front of the mirror and look at yourself. Without judging, simply observe yourself from head to toe. Look at yourself from the sides; now turn around and look at yourself from the back. *Remember, don't judge!* Just become familiar with your physical body for a few minutes each day. Do this every morning or evening until you're quite comfortable gazing at your body without criticism. Become as familiar with your whole body as you are with the back of your hand.

Now, as you continue your daily mirror exercise, examine each part of your body. Look carefully at your face, your arms, your chest, back, legs, and so on. Say to yourself: "I accept and love all of me." At first you might feel a bit silly, but keep at it until you can look in the mirror and genuinely feel a comfortable acceptance of the body you have. Any time a judgmental thought creeps in ("I have thunder thighs" or "I'm not very muscular"), let that thought pass by. Ignore it. Then say to yourself: "This is the way I am. I like every part of me." Don't ever fall into the trap of disliking yourself because you don't like a particular part of your body.

Once you've accepted your body and feel at ease with the way you are now, you can begin to make any changes you want. If you feel uncoordinated, take a dance class, sign up for tennis or yoga lessons—anything that will help you learn to control and coordinate your physical movements. Approach any class with this goal firmly in mind: "I'm here to learn how to work with my body; I'm *not* here to become an expert dancer or tennis pro."

Regular exercise does more than keep you physically fit. Even attaining modest exercise goals will help build your self-esteem. A colleague of mine is our department's biggest exercise fan. She confided to me that when she first began her exercise program she could run only half a block. Now she can run two miles and cycle for fifteen. Her sense of accomplishment and pride literally makes her glow.

Many communities offer adult education classes on a wide variety of topics. Use your community resources to help you make the most of what you have. Take a class on how to use accessories, have your colors analyzed, take a voice training class. Approach those aspects of your outer appearance that you'd like to change with a sense of fun and experimentation. Don't strive for perfection—simply enjoy treating the outer you with care and respect.

While you're practicing your daily mirror exercise and learning to love and accept your outer image, you should also be working on your inner self. Let's tackle this by looking first at how the typical shy person thinks.

THE PSYCHOLOGY OF SHYNESS

Think of one recent success and one recent failure you've experienced, and then ask yourself who or what was responsible for each. Do you take credit for your success or do you pass it off as circumstantial, due to someone else, or just plain good luck? Do you blame yourself for the failure?

It's typical for shy people to foist the credit for success on everyone else while assigning the blame for failure on themselves. By contrast, most self-assured people take credit for their successes and blame their failures on circumstances. Why do shy people reverse this normal thinking pattern? Why is it so difficult for shy people to accept personal credit for positive results?

One explanation is that blaming yourself for failure and giving credit for success to outside circumstances fits in with the internal view you already have of yourself.[7] If you feel worthless and inept, then failures must be your fault. And, obviously, any success can't be to your credit because you're worthless and inept—how could you be responsible for a "win"? If you claim success as your own and brush off your failures, you create an inconsistency with the internal view you have of yourself. Inconsistencies are hard to accept. It's a peculiarly human trait to line up our perception of events so that they match our internal evaluation, even if that evaluation is negative.

Studies have shown that shy people maintain their negative self-images despite evidence to the contrary. Psychologist Stephen Franzoi of the University of California asked shy and non-shy people to check off from a list those adjectives that they felt described them best.[8] He then had a friend of each participant check off from an identical list the adjectives that he or she felt described the friend in the study. His results showed three items of particular interest.

First, the shy people tended to have lower self-esteem than the non-shy participants. Second, in describing themselves the shy participants checked off more negative adjectives than their friends did. Third, when confronted with their friends' more positive evaluations, the shy people refused to believe the positive appraisals. They just couldn't accept the good feedback about themselves.

Try a home version of Franzoi's study. First, in your self-development notebook write down all your positive characteristics, all the things that you like about yourself. Next, write out this sentence on the top of two or three sheets of paper: "What I like about you is that you are . . ." Then ask two or three people whom you like and trust to finish the sentence. You can tell them that you're working on feeling better about yourself and that you'd like to know what it is about you that they particularly value. When you've collected their responses, compare them with your own list. How many of the descriptions overlap with yours? How many are different? How do you feel about the descriptions that weren't on your list—can you accept them easily as a friend's honest evaluation of you?

Shy people also have excellent memories for all their faults and for all the most embarrassing episodes in their lives. When asked to list both their positive and negative personality traits and then recall them later, shy people remembered more of their negative traits than did non-shy participants.[9] Even more telling, the shy participants also recalled fewer of their self-described positive traits than did their affable counterparts.

Here's a little experiment for you to do. Sit down with your self-development notebook and write down a memory of a time when you felt proud of yourself. When you've finished with that, write down a memory of a time when you felt embarrassed.

I once asked a group of college students to do this same experiment. Interestingly, the shy students' accounts of their humiliations were longer and more detailed than those of the non-shy students, just as their recollections of their triumphs were shorter. How do your descriptions compare with those of my students? Was your description of your embarrassing episode full of detail that the description of your proud memory lacked?

Focusing on your faults, reserving your most vivid descriptions for a sort of mental hall of shame, is a surefire antidote to improving your self-image. You can't feel good about yourself if you can't readily acknowledge your virtues. You short-circuit the process of building high self-esteem by rejecting positive self-acceptance and by beating up on yourself for failures.

Fear of rejection plays a similarly damaging role in shy people's negative perspective. Whenever there is a risk of rejection, shy people protect themselves by withdrawing from a social activity, keeping their thoughts to themselves, pretending to agree with others rather than make waves or provoke disapproval.[10] If we think of social life as a game, we can see that shy people don't usually play to win; they play not to lose.

Brandon, a burly man of thirty-nine, doesn't have many friends. "I'm afraid to approach people because of fear of rejection," he says. "I can rationalize with myself and tell myself people aren't standing in judgment of me, but I can't seem to overcome it." Brandon's fears aren't totally unfounded. The reality is that we *are* judged by the people around us, just as we judge them. But the fear of rejection becomes irrational when it stops us from getting out and making the effort to be friendly.

Rejection doesn't mean we're worthless, yet shy people accept rejection as proof positive of their worthlessness. You can't realistically expect *everyone* to like you. You *will* be rejected by some people, and as you become more socially active you yourself will occasionally reject friendly overtures from others. People don't hit it off every time.

Every now and then you'll encounter someone who's just having a bad day. There's nothing wrong with you—the person's just not in a frame of mind to be friendly. He or she may just have been chewed out by their boss or had a fight with their spouse or experienced a day when "everything went wrong." Yet time and again, shy people feel rejected in this type of situation. Somehow another person's ill humor is their fault. "What did I do wrong? Did I say something I shouldn't have?" No, it's none of those things. Don't automatically assume that you're the cause of someone's bad mood, whether that person is an acquaintance, friend, or lover.

Hoping for acceptance from all people at all times is an unrealistic all-or-nothing kind of thinking: "Either everyone likes me or no one likes me." There are very few people in our lives who even come close to offering us unconditional acceptance and/or love. Those are special relationships and as such deserve to be cherished for the rarities that they are.

CHANGING YOUR ATTITUDE
THINK LIKE A WINNER!

As we said earlier, each of us begins to feel self-conscious as we experience physical changes and assume new roles in late childhood and early adolescence. That self-consciousness may continue to haunt us into adulthood, when life deals out both general and specific circumstances that undermine our self-esteem and reinforce our feelings of shyness.

The way you carry yourself and judge your attractiveness usually reflects your inner feelings of worthlessness. Along with that, faulty thinking commands your mental processes. Your negative self-image is reinforced by concentrating on the negatives, by denying yourself credit for your successes, and by a deep-seated fear of rejection.

It's time for you to stop thinking like a loser and reprogram yourself to *think like a winner.*

Is your glass half full or half empty? Studies of optimistic and pessimistic people have shown great differences in the way these two extremes comprehend the world around them.[11] Optimists handle stress better than their pessimistic counterparts, responding to failure by formulating a plan of action and readily asking other people for help and advice. The optimist takes a "can-do" approach to life. The pessimist, on the other hand, is likely to assume that there is nothing he can do to change things for the better and the best policy is not even to try. The optimist controls his world; he views setbacks as events that can be remedied with the correct approach. Optimists make an attempt to change. Pessimists, however, allow events to determine their fate. They regard setbacks as the result of a personal deficit—a deficit that will follow them throughout life.

Shy people are pessimists. They expect the worst to happen, they focus on their setbacks, and they tell themselves that they'll never get it right.[12] Outgoing people are optimists. They emphasize positive outcomes, seek help from others, and when things don't work, they see setbacks as temporary detours from their ultimate triumph.

If you are a shy person, one of the best things you can do for yourself is to turn your pessimistic thinking around. Don't be unrealistic, but go ahead and try on the optimist's thinking cap. Let me give you some examples of pessimistic versus optimistic thinking.

Pessimistic Thinking	Optimistic Thinking
My first day on the job . . . I'll look stupid because I don't know everything and people probably won't like me.	My first day on the job! This will be great—I'll learn new skills and meet more new people.
What's going on? I can't figure out these numbers! I knew I'd fail at this.	What's happening? I can't make heads or tails out of these numbers. Oh well, I'll see if Bob can give me some help.
Here I am shopping alone again. I'll bet every person I pass wonders why I'm by myself.	I love shopping alone. I set my own pace and go to whatever stores I want to.
What if Dr. Samuels asks if I still smoke? I'm always so nervous around doctors, I'll probably sound like a babbling idiot making excuses.	Oh boy, Dr. Samuels is going to give me another lecture about smoking when I go in for my physical. Better prepare myself!
Why is she so curious about my hobbies? There's nothing interesting about me. What'll I say?	She's interested in me! She mentioned art galleries, so I'll tell her about the class I took on modern art.

Get the idea? Remember that I said in Chapter 1 that you need to learn to be an observer of your own behavior? You'll also need to learn to monitor your own thoughts. Think about the last day or two and see if you can remember any of the negative thoughts you had during your daily encounters with people. Write them down in the left-hand column below, or in your self-development notebook, and think about how you can rephrase them into optimistic statements. Jot down these new statements in the right-hand column.

MY RECENT PESSIMISTIC   MY RECENT OPTIMISTIC
THOUGHTS   THOUGHTS

Every time you catch yourself thinking like a pessimist, immediately rephrase your thought into an optimistic one. Get in the habit of catching your negative thoughts and quickly turning them around before you sink into the quagmire of pessimism and low self-esteem.

CULTIVATING SELF-ACCEPTANCE

Building up your self-esteem takes time, and no one learns to like himself overnight. Most people's negative thoughts propel themselves with a kind of self-perpetuating centrifugal force, so reversing the direction of your thoughts requires dogged, daily practice until the practice becomes habit and the habit becomes second nature.

You have to say to yourself, "I'm the person responsible for having a better day today, a better week this week." With practice, you can learn to feel good about who you are. To get you started, try this exercise. In your self-development notebook, finish the following sentence in as many ways as you can:

"I'm a person who likes _____."

Since you might draw a blank at first, I'll share with you some of my answers to this statement.

I'm a person who likes . . .

- learning new things and telling other people about them.
- taking long walks in the country.
- watching Australian movies.
- listening to music from the '60s.
- cooking out on the backyard grill.
- spending time with my family.
- traveling to foreign countries.
- collecting Haitian art.

Another exercise you can use to improve your general emotional attitude toward yourself is one given to me by a counselor many years ago. To counter my depression at the end of a romantic relationship, my counselor had me look myself in the mirror every morning and say, "Good morning. I like you. You are my best friend." Sounds silly, doesn't it?

At first, although I repeated these words to myself each morning, I found it hard to say them with any conviction. But as the mornings went by, I began to feel better and better. Slowly but surely I was reprogramming the way I thought about myself.

I think that you could add something to this exercise. Go back to your earlier assignment—when you listed your positive qualities and collected other people's listings of your good points. To the three sentences I learned to say to myself, add a fourth one: "You are _____." Fill in that space with whatever positive description you found hard to accept from your friends' assessments of you.

Keep saying it to yourself until you reprogram yourself to believe it. Then move on to the next one on the list that you found difficult to believe.

UPS AND DOWNS

Feeling great about yourself is exhilarating. The only problem is that we all have our ups and downs. After a period of finally getting in touch with all the wonderful things there are about you, you may suddenly encounter a down day. Please don't think that you've lost everything you've worked so hard to gain. Don't let yourself fall victim to negativity and pessimism again. You didn't fail. You're just having a bad day.

On down days treat yourself to a pick-me-up. Here are some suggestions:

- Use the relaxation exercises you learned in Chapter 2 to calm yourself and regain your inner tranquility.
- If you feel that you've really made a blunder in something you said or did, learn from that mistake. Visualize how you'd do it differently next time, but don't dwell on what you did wrong.
- Think about all the positive things you've accomplished lately and give yourself a pat on the back.
- It's easy to fall back into your old negative thinking habits, so remember to use your optimistic thinking exercise to chase away your self-deprecating thoughts.
- Look back at your friends' "What I like about you . . ." lists and bask in the glow of your strengths.
- When life is hectic on a down day, call a time-out. Take five or ten minutes for yourself and regroup. Find a quiet place to sit or take a quick walk and plan a strategy for making the rest of the day better.
- At home at the end of a down day, do whatever you want to get back in touch with the positive side of yourself. Curl up with a book; soak in a long, hot bath; prepare your favorite dinner; call a friend; refuse to answer the phone when it rings; go to bed early knowing that tomorrow things will be better.

Use any or all of these strategies to nip feelings of low self-esteem in the bud. Don't give in to negative thoughts and don't replay a bad day over and over again to yourself. Keep working on your esteem-building exercises. Perseverance will pay off in the end.

As your self-esteem improves, you'll find your shyness beginning to fade. Approaching new people, talking to your boss or other authority figures—these will seem easier when you feel good about yourself. Going to new places or joining in on a group activity won't feel quite so intimidating. Instead of automatically assuming that others won't like you, you'll feel confident that you're a likable person whom others want to spend time with.

CHAPTER 4

The Self-Absorption Trap

There's a wonderful scene in the movie *Annie Hall* when Diane Keaton and Woody Allen are having a drink on her apartment balcony just after they've first met. Subtitles flash what Keaton and Allen are each thinking while they talk. Woody begins by asking Keaton about the family photographs he's seen hanging on her wall. (Their private thoughts are indicated in parentheses.)[1]

ALLEN: So, did you do those photographs in there or what?

KEATON: Yeah, yeah. I sort of dabble around, you know. (I dabble? Listen to me—what a jerk.)

ALLEN: They're wonderful. You know they have a . . . they have a quality. (You are a great-looking girl.)

KEATON: Well, I would like to take a serious photography course.
(He probably thinks I'm a yo-yo.)

ALLEN: Photography is interesting because you know it's a new art form and
a set of aesthetic criteria has not emerged yet.
(I wonder what she looks like naked.)

KEATON: Aesthetic criteria . . . You mean whether it's a good photo or not?
(I'm not smart enough for him. Hang in there.)

ALLEN: The medium enters in as a condition of the art form itself . . .
(I don't know what I'm saying—she senses I'm shallow.)

KEATON: Well . . . Well, to me, I . . . I mean it's . . . it's all instinctive.
You know, I mean I just try to feel it, you know, I try to get a sense of it
and not think about it so much.
(God, I hope he doesn't turn out to be a shmuck like the others.)

ALLEN: Still, you need a set of aesthetic guidelines to put it in social perspective, I think.
(Christ, I sound like FM radio. Relax.)

This brilliant scene is a superb example of the self-absorption
trap. The shy Keaton thinks she sounds like a jerk and a yo-yo,
believes she's not as smart as Allen, and finally bolsters herself with
the thought that Woody could turn out to be a shmuck anyway.
Allen is distracted by his sexual attraction to Keaton, and then
begins riding hard on himself for babbling away and sounding like
a phony authority.

Everyone wants to make a good impression. But when *all* your
attention is focused on how you're performing and on guessing
what other people are thinking about you, it becomes counter-
productive. You feel self-conscious because you're afraid you'll fail
to put on a good show. Acutely aware of yourself as a social being,
you begin watching everything you do and say, noticing discrepan-
cies between your actual behavior and your ideal behavior. Your

self-confidence plummets and you find yourself caught in the self-absorption trap.

WHAT ARE YOU THINKING ABOUT?

A study my colleague Lisa Melchior and I conducted revealed some very interesting information about self-absorption.[2] We introduced pairs of shy and non-shy people and left them alone to talk about anything they wanted for five minutes. After they were through, we asked each person what they were thinking about during their time together. *The non-shy participants were concerned about themselves twenty percent of the time, but the shy participants were self-absorbed forty percent of the time.* The shy people worried about their social and conversational skills instead of focusing on the other person. To make matters worse, their thoughts, like those of Annie Hall, were mostly negative.

Making lively conversation and being at ease socially won't happen when you're constantly evaluating yourself. Because you're so preoccupied with your own thoughts and worries, you may miss other people's cues that you're doing just fine. You may be doing better than you think you are. Shy people need to spend less time paying attention to themselves and more time paying attention to the people around them.

ARE SHY PEOPLE SELFISH?

After being interviewed about my work on shyness in *U.S. News & World Report*, I received a letter from a reader of that magazine asking me that question:

Dear Professor Cheek,
*   When I was growing up I suffered from shyness. My mother, in an effort to get me out of this shyness, kept telling me that shyness was a form of selfishness. As I have never heard or read that shyness is a form of selfishness, I have to conclude that my mother was sadly mistaken and was perhaps a little desperate to get me over this shyness. What is your opinion of all this?*

*   Barbara M.*

Sometimes others do believe that shy people are selfish, but it's really a misconception. When I studied this aspect of shyness, I found that shy people can *appear* to be selfish. Those whose trouble is mostly with anxious thoughts and worries *are* self-absorbed and self-preoccupied.[3] When you're engrossed in your own thoughts, you don't give much attention to the people around you. Since other people don't know what's running through your mind (they're not mind readers), they may sometimes interpret your behavior as selfish.

WHAT OTHERS THINK OF SHY PEOPLE

What do socially self-confident people think about shy people? They simply don't understand that you're immobilized by anxious thoughts and worries. They believe that you fail in social situations because you're not putting any effort into being more outgoing. And the reason they think this way has to do with their own way of viewing the world. When non-shy people experience interpersonal success, they credit their own personality traits and abilities for that success. When they meet with failure, non-shy people blame an external cause. For example, they tell themselves they tried, but the other person wasn't friendly. Naturally, they believe everyone thinks the way they do. So when they're with a shy person who can't cope socially, they figure the person is not using his or her abilities to handle the situation.[4]

Researchers have discovered that shy people believe their social failures result from a lack of interpersonal skills. When Lynn Alden, of the University of British Columbia, conducted a study in which participants were sometimes given positive feedback and sometimes negative feedback for their social performance, the shy people believed the negative feedback but doubted the accuracy of the positive feedback![5]

When you take credit for social failures, believing that the fault lies within yourself, you're perpetuating the feeling that you'll always be a social failure. But you're wrong. You're depriving yourself of positive social feedback and blaming yourself unnecessarily.

As you begin to change your attitude through the exercises outlined later in this chapter, look for small improvements in your
behavior—not dramatic changes—and give yourself a pat on the
back for every effort you make to be less shy. Don't allow yourself
to fall into the vicious circle of self-blame.

A DANGEROUS QUICK FIX

Erica, twenty-four, has always been shy around other people, yet
she's anxious to establish an easy camaraderie with her acquaintances. Unfortunately, she's taking the easy way out in her private
battle with shyness: "I feel self-conscious just walking down the
street," she says. "Shyness has also made me a problem drinker—it
seems I can talk better when I'm loaded."

The one readily available "self-help" drug for reducing anxiety
and self-absorption is alcohol.[6] Alcohol masks anxiety and quickly
reduces inhibitions. Yet this quick fix is a killer: Alcoholism can
destroy you and your life; and when you drive drunk you're a lethal
weapon behind the wheel. Alcohol is ultimately an ineffective and
harmful coping strategy. There's nothing wrong with a little social
drinking, but you can learn to cope better through other methods.

AN INFORMATION-PROCESSING MODEL

There's always so much going on in the world that it's impossible
to give meaning to everything we see and hear. What we do is
selectively take in information that seems relevant to us. Remember being in a crowded room and suddenly hearing your name
mentioned from across the room? Despite the buzz of conversation going on around you, your brain recognizes something relevant to you—your name. Psychologists call this the "cocktail party
phenomenon." Even while we're engrossed in a conversation, our
ears constantly monitor all the voices around us. Only when something significant is picked up do we immediately become alert to a
conversation taking place at some distance from us.

Think of your mind as being like a computer program, which is set up to receive information in a certain order and only from certain parts of the keyboard. If you enter information or commands in the wrong place, the computer rejects it. We're a little bit like computers in the way we recognize the information that daily assaults our eyes and ears.

As a shy person troubled with negative thoughts and worries, your mind keeps running the "social failure" program. Each time you're in a social situation, your cunning brain selects and stores away all the information that fits your program, stockpiling it for ready reference. Information telling you that you're a social success is disregarded. It doesn't fit into your program. It's rejected—it doesn't compute.

When you recall the events of the day at work or an evening out, what do you focus on? The items stored away in your information-processing model, your internal computer program. In acutely embarrassing detail you remember all the things you did and said that were wrong, confirming your belief that you're socially inept.

But your mind is storing more than information, as the psychologist Gordon H. Bower has theorized.[7] Feelings *and* their accompanying event reside in our memory. When we're in a happy mood it's easier to recall happy times, and conversely when we're feeling sad, the memories of sad events are easily recalled. Bower also believes that emotion acts as a selective filter in our perceptions of people and situations. For instance, when we're anticipating a happy time we easily perceive those things that confirm the event is indeed a happy one. But when the "shyness filter" is in place, we note only the lags in conversation, the pattern of the floor tile, and the distressing moments of time spent alone between conversational partners.

Now let's apply Bower's ideas to shyness. Picture yourself with your shyness filter on. You arrive at your company's midsummer picnic. Your anxiety thermometer starts to rise dramatically. Why don't you recognize most of the people here? Because your company has suddenly doubled in size with the addition of coworkers' friends, spouses, and children. Frantically your eyes dart around, looking for a familiar face. Oh, there's Bob from purchasing, you say to yourself. But wait, he's talking to someone you don't know. Your anxiety level shoots up another two degrees. Should you walk over there and join them? What if you interrupt a private conversation? You don't know Bob all that well—maybe he wouldn't appreciate you sauntering over and intruding. You're frozen, unable to figure out where to move. Then the loudspeaker blares: Line up! Lunch is served! The crowd moves toward the food table. As the smell of hamburgers and hot dogs on the grill wafts your way, you think, "I don't know anybody here. Who am I going to talk to? Who am I going to eat with? I'll feel silly lining up for a hamburger without someone in the line to talk to. This is going to be a terrible afternoon. Maybe I should leave now. Oh, why did I ever come to this thing?"

Later, when you look back on that afternoon, you recall not just what you did at the picnic, but also all the feelings you had while you were there. All the doubt and anxiety you endured, all your premonitions that this wasn't going to be the high point of your social calendar. You feel the heat of embarrassment again as you recall the awful moment when you dumped your potato salad right in Bob's lap and called Nancy's husband by the wrong name. With a pang of loneliness, you feel again the isolation of sitting a little bit apart from everyone else during the volleyball game. Your shyness filter did its job—it selected out all the events of the day that confirmed your worst fears.

But what would happen if you changed your emotional filter? What if you looked forward to the company picnic instead of dreading it? Instead of seeing a large group of people you don't recognize, you'd see some fellow employees and some interesting new people to meet. Later, when recalling the events of the day, you'd focus your memories on the funny joke you told your boss. You'd recall with pleasure meeting Nancy's husband and determine to do better at remembering people's names the next time you're introduced to a new group. And instead of sitting off to one side during the volleyball game, you'd sit closer to the other spectators and try your hand at making small talk. All in all, you'd look back on the day with pleasure, an outing well enjoyed.

When your internal program is set up for social failure and your shyness filter is in place, it's no wonder you're focused on anything but the situation in hand. All your attention is turned inward, with the occasional scan for bits and pieces of conversation, for the looks and gestures from others that fit your social failure program. Your mood and mind are ready for another disappointing social encounter.

Your social failure program is based on a set of beliefs that support and nurture it. Those beliefs, in turn, switch on your inner voice, the one that shouts, "You're doing it again, you're messing up!"

Now that you're aware of how much negative programming is affecting your life, it's possible to change the program to create positive experiences and memories. But before I detail the exercises for accomplishing this change, it's important to discuss the impact of irrational thinking and beliefs on shy people.

IRRATIONAL THINKING AND BELIEFS

Shy people hold many irrational beliefs about themselves and the social situations they find themselves in.[8] Irrational beliefs progress to catastrophic predictions. They're based on the following three premises:

1. All people must like and approve of me at all times; if anyone doesn't, I won't be able to bear it.
2. I must be socially perfect in order to think of myself as worthy; if my behavior is flawed and things go awry, I'll know who to blame—myself.
3. If situations don't proceed as I think they should, it's my fault.

I talked about Premise 1 in the last chapter, but let me emphasize again how unrealistic it is to expect that *everyone* will like and approve of you. It isn't a disaster if someone doesn't like you. To believe otherwise can make a catastrophe out of everyday experience.

Premise 2 means that your standards of performance are too high. There's nothing wrong with high personal standards, but nobody's perfect. Feeling like a fool or a failure is self-defeating. The worst part of Premise 2 is when shy people draw a general conclusion from a single incident. For example, you make an awkward comment at a dinner party and you think you've ruined the evening for yourself and everyone else.

Premise 3 assumes that you have total control. That's a serious mistake. None of us do. You aren't powerful enough to determine the outcome of every situation. You can do your best to create positive social situations, but to blame yourself because an occasion is less than perfect denies other people's impact. They too contribute to the success or failure of social encounters.

DISPUTING YOUR IRRATIONAL THOUGHTS

Whenever you begin your tirade of irrational thoughts, ask yourself these four questions:

1. How likely or true is that?
2. How catastrophic is that even if it happens?
3. What is true about the situation?
4. What is more important to believe?

Let's look at an example of disputing irrational thoughts. Landon, fifty-five, is the owner of a bookstore where I frequently find myself on Sunday afternoons. He's a very shy man, who confessed to me one day that he couldn't walk into a crowded room by himself. "It'd be awful," he said, leaning over a stack of books he'd piled up near the cash register. "I always feel no one will want to talk to me and I'll be left standing alone." He was clearly upset as he talked, and I offered a few words of advice about how to dispute his irrational thoughts. Here's what I told him to say to himself:

1. It is *physically* possible for me to walk into a room by myself. It's my negative thoughts that stop me from doing it. It's also very unlikely that not one single person would talk to me—I think I'm exaggerating here.
2. If I refuse to enter a room with lots of people in it, the worst that can happen is that I'll miss an opportunity to possibly enjoy myself or learn something new. Even if no one did talk to me, it wouldn't be the end of the world.
3. What is true about this situation is that almost everybody feels the same way about walking into a crowded room. I'm not the only one who feels nervous about it.
4. It's more important for me to believe in myself—that I *can* do it. Other people there will probably be feeling a little uncomfortable too, and that's one way to start up a conversation with someone! It's also important for me to remember that I'm an interesting person who is learning how to be more relaxed in social situations.

Be careful when you dispute your irrational thoughts: You don't want to create mere rationalizations. If in step 4 Landon were to say, "I don't care whether other people talk to me or not—if they can't see that I'm an interesting person, then it's their problem, not mine," he'd be rationalizing. Landon's goal is realistic: He wants other people to like him. He wants to learn how to be more comfortable in social settings and to recognize that a minor setback is not a catastrophe. That's also realistic.[9]

Some shy people have said to me that they have trouble naming their irrational thoughts. If you're having this difficulty, ask yourself specifically what you are feeling. Then move on to why you're feeling that way. For example, if you're feeling anxious, ask yourself "Why am I feeling anxious?" You might answer "Because I don't want to write the monthly business report." The question "Why don't I want to write the report?" will then lead you to your irrational thought: "I don't think I can do it."

If you're still having difficulties once you've identified your irrational thought or thoughts, continue by asking yourself these five questions:

1. What behavior supports my irrational thought?
   (Procrastinating! Working on other things that could really wait until after the report is done.)
2. What evidence is there for my belief?
   (None. I wrote the report last month.)
3. What beliefs would support my preferred behavior?
   (I wrote a good report last month, so I know I can do it again this month.)
4. What will happen if I don't change my thoughts and behavior?
   (I'll still have to write the report, but I'll have wasted valuable time trying to convince myself that I can't do it.)
5. What might happen if I do change my thoughts and behavior?
   (I might approach the task with more enthusiasm and get the job done in record time and with greater satisfaction.)

Next, take out your self-development notebook and review your shyness situations from Chapter 1. Beginning at the bottom of the list—your least fearful situation—write out what your irrational thoughts are about that situation. Then dispute them. Work your way up your list and see how many of your shy situations evoke the same irrational belief or fear. Whenever a circumstance pops up that sets your anxiety thermometer shooting up, stop and listen to your inner thoughts. Talk right back to them. Cut them off at the pass before they get the better of you. This may seem like a long, tedious exercise. But it's vital if you want to make real progress against your shyness.

Here are a couple of tips to improve your chances of working effectively at this exercise. First of all, don't try to complete this assignment all in one afternoon. Set up a goal plan to tackle one situation each day or every other day or in whatever time frame your schedule allows. Second, have faith in the exercise. It really does work. Psychologists have conducted what are called "outcome studies," which compare the effectiveness of different treatment methods. These studies have shown that there are real improvements when people work diligently at restructuring their attitudes toward situations.[10]

Irrational thoughts and beliefs provide the foundation for negative self-statements. Therefore, chipping away at them is one step in changing your program.

NEGATIVE SELF-STATEMENTS

"I'm such a social klutz . . . Why am I always doing the wrong thing? . . . They're probably laughing at me behind my back . . . I can't think of anything to say! I'm always so tongue-tied at parties, people will soon stop inviting me . . . I don't stand a chance for the promotion, I'm not good enough . . . He probably thinks I'm weird . . . I better not speak up, I'll only make a fool of myself . . . I can't just walk up and talk to him, he doesn't even know I'm alive . . ."

Shy people are particularly prone to filling their minds with statements of this kind.[11] All deal with self-perception and all are negative. Sometimes you might be aware of your inner negative thoughts; at other times they may parade through your mind without your really being aware of them. And while you're filling your mind with specific negative statements, your negative feelings about yourself become generalized into the fear that others won't like you.

What we say to ourselves profoundly affects how we behave and how we perceive social situations. It's important that you learn to monitor your inner critic and take defensive action against it. The key to doing this is positive self-statements, which help eliminate those negative thoughts and reprograms you for social success.

MOVING FROM NEGATIVE
TO POSITIVE SELF-STATEMENTS

Negative self-statements lead to a fear of rejection that is often self-fulfilling. Here's how it sounds when an upcoming job interview is involved:

NEGATIVE SELF-STATEMENTS	FEAR OF REJECTION
They probably won't want to hire me.	I'm afraid I'll never find a good job.

I'm not comfortable during job interviews, so I'm sure to bungle it.	If I louse up this interview, I'll never regain my confidence.
I'll probably sound like I don't know what I'm talking about.	I'd be horrified if I couldn't be articulate.
I'll feel awkward and dumb; the interviewer will wonder why I ever applied for the job.	I'll feel awful if they don't offer me the job.

Thoughts like these keep us from putting our best foot forward. Positive self-regard, on the other hand, is the consequence of positive self-statements. Contrast the above negative way of thinking with the positive approach that follows:

POSITIVE SELF-STATEMENTS	POSITIVE SELF-REGARD
This company may be very interested in the skills I have to offer.	The worst that can happen is that my skills don't match what they're looking for.
With each interview I become more relaxed and improve my interviewing techniques.	Every interview gets me closer to finding the job I want.
I'll emphasize my strengths for the job and how my education fits in.	Even if I don't know the answer to a question, it's not a disaster.
I'll keep positive about myself and focus on whether I'd be right for the job.	If I'm not offered the job, I'll just keep interviewing until I find the right one.

Check your self-development notebook, look at your list of shy situations, and again choose a situation that's ranked near the bottom of the list and that you encounter regularly. The next time you're in that situation, don't do anything different at first. Simply monitor your thoughts and the conclusions you draw from them about how you'll handle the situation. Write down all your negative self-statements and the false generalizations they engender. Then rewrite your negative self-statements into positive self-statements and your negative generalizations into positive, effective coping strategies. The next time you're in that situation and you hear those negative self-statements pop up, immediately redirect your thoughts to the positive ones you've written down. When you find yourself in your shyness situation and your positive self-statements surface automatically, move on to the next situation on your list and tackle that one. Keep working up your list until you've reached the top.

Remember: You're not trying to change any of your *behavior* with this exercise. You're simply changing the way you *think* about yourself in your shyness situations. No one will even guess that you're quietly working on overcoming your shyness. This is a method that's stood the test of outcome studies. It really *will* help you get rid of negative thoughts and approach social situations with greater confidence.

DECENTERING—CHANGING THE WAY YOU ACT

As you begin learning to talk to yourself in a supportive way, you also need to learn how to direct your attention away from yourself and toward other people. Decentering is a technique you can use to develop your skills in observing, listening, responding, and initiating conversation.[12] Practiced in social situations, this technique makes it all but impossible for you to become self-absorbed. After all, you can't focus on yourself and other people at the same time.

The easiest way to explain decentering is through an example. Renee is a twenty-eight-year-old technical writer working for a large bank in San Diego. While she's a whiz at writing up numbers into annual reports and the bank's other financial literature, she's tongue-tied when it comes to socializing with her work mates. Worried that she won't be liked by everyone, she keeps constant tabs on herself. Instead of joining the gang on Friday evenings at the local bar, she trudges home to her empty apartment. But now Renee has decided to make a change in her life and she's begun keeping a self-development notebook.

Looking through her shy situations list, Renee selects the midmorning coffee break as the best situation with which to begin her decentering exercises—it's less threatening than the noisy laughter and ribald conversation at the group's favorite bar.

When the people in her department gather around the vending machines for their morning coffee and pastry, Renee's first act is simply to observe everyone (without staring), watching their postures, mannerisms, facial expression, and how well each person maintains eye contact. When she gets home in the evening, she writes down her observations. Christopher, she's noticed, has a habit of rubbing his forehead when he's thinking about his answer to a question. Shannon looks everyone right in the eye, as bold as can be. Cory would never make a good poker player—Renee can almost guess what he's going to say just by looking at the expression on his face. Anytime a negative thought about herself creeps into her mind, Renee redirects her mind toward her observation exercise.

After she becomes comfortable in her role as an observer, Renee moves on to the next step—listening. Now when she arrives home at night, she writes down as much as she can remember of the daily coffee-break conversation. Increasingly, it's difficult for her to focus on herself. It requires a lot of attention to hear and remember what the morning's conversation was. When she looks through several days' jottings of the conversations she's recorded, she finds that the people she once feared are everyday people talking about everyday, mundane topics. Few of them are brilliant conversationalists, yet they're still well-liked and enjoy their contact with each other. Now she realizes that she's just as capable as her fellow workers to carry on conversations.

The next stage is harder—it requires every ounce of her attention. Renee now must learn how to integrate the group's gestures, facial expressions, and tone of voice with the content of their conversation. Christopher, she discovers, rubs his forehead only when he's going to disagree with someone else's question or comment. She finds that Shannon's voice drops a whole octave when she's mad about something. Cory's facial expressions play over his face even while he's listening, and become very noticeable when he's excited about anything—a new company program, who won the baseball game last night, or the plot of the latest spy novel he's been reading.

Before she knows it, Renee has learned how to become an active listener. She feels comfortable joining the coffee break, and she's bursting with ideas and thoughts on the daily conversations. She's become so proficient in decentering that she rarely has a negative thought or worry about herself. All her attention is on the other people and the conversation.

It's easy now for Renee to join in the conversation—for the first time she's actually hearing what's being said. She's learned her coworkers' habits so well that she can tell when Cory's feeling down, or when Shannon's nervous about something. Reading their cues, Renee can always open up a conversation with, "Cory, you look down today, didn't the new IRA brochures sell with the marketing people?" Or, "Shannon, stop tapping your foot and tell me what's going on!" A conversation is born.

That's how decentering works: observing, listening, integrating your observations with the content of the conversation, and using what you've learned to start future conversations. Believe me, it beats sitting there in your own world focused on yourself. Just remember to start practicing decentering with your least fearful shyness situation and gradually work up to your hardest one. One step at a time!

IF YOU'RE STILL PLAGUED WITH WORRIES . . .

If you're faithfully working on disputing your irrational beliefs, countering your negative self-statements with positive ones, and practicing decentering, but are still finding it difficult to stop worrying, here are two exercises I'd like you to try.

One way to control your worrying is through a method devised by Thomas Borkovec, a psychologist at Pennsylvania State University. Describing his work in the December 1985 issue of *Psychology Today* magazine, Borkovec adapted his exercise from learning theory, which holds that behaviors are associated with the situations in which they take place.[13] For example, if a cigarette smoker lights up after every meal, every time he sits down to write a letter or pay bills, and every time he's on the telephone, smoking becomes associated with all those activities. But, if a smoker only allowed himself to have a cigarette on the front porch, then gradually he'd begin to disassociate smoking from all those other situations. His daily cigarette consumption would soon decrease dramatically.

Since you can worry in anticipation of a social encounter, worry while you're involved in the situation, and worry about it afterward, it can become a full-time preoccupation. Borkovec suggests *limiting* the conditions in which you allow yourself to worry through these five rules:

1. Closely observe your thinking during the day and learn to identify the first pangs of anxiety.
2. Establish a half-hour "worry period" for the same time and same place each day.
3. As soon as you catch yourself worrying, postpone it until your worry period.
4. Replace your worrisome thoughts with focused attention on the task at hand or on anything else in your immediate environment.
5. Use your daily worry period to think intensively about your anxieties.

Borkovec's five rules isolate worry to one specific time and place. In his research he found that people successfully reduced the amount of time they spent worrying each day when they used this technique.

If you try this method, I'd suggest you follow up with a workout on disputing the irrational thoughts or negative self-statements that undoubtedly surfaced during your worry period.

IMAGINE YOUR WAY TO A BETTER YOU

Here's another way to combat worries. Instead of focusing on your current anxiety, visualize yourself as you'd like to be. Go ahead—imagine yourself as a witty and articulate person, see yourself confidently walking into a roomful of strangers.

Hazel Markus of the University of Michigan calls this visualizing our "possible selves."[14] In a study she conducted with Ann Ruvolo, Markus asked students to imagine themselves in the future —either as highly successful or as failures. After their imaging, the students were given a difficult task to perform. Those who had imagined themselves as successful in the future performed much better than those who imagined themselves as failures. Markus believes that our possible selves may serve as powerful motivators for our present actions and actually help guide our behavior.

KEEP UP A POSITIVE MENTAL ATTITUDE

As you work with the exercises in this chapter, look for small improvements in your thoughts and behavior. Give yourself cycles of positive feedback for positive outcomes, and you'll find that changes come more easily. If you don't meet with success the first time round, don't blame yourself: You're in the process of retraining your thought patterns, and that takes time. When you feel discouraged, say to yourself, "I'm learning not to be so self-absorbed," and push ahead. It took you a long time to fall into the rut you feel stuck in now, so be realistic about giving yourself an abundance of time to work your way out of it.

CHAPTER 5

Developing Your Social Skills

I magine learning to ride a bicycle for the first time at age thirty, forty, or fifty. Just about everyone learns how to ride in child-hood, so you'd expect some awkwardness, even feel a little foolish if you took a spill now and then. Mastering social skills is like riding a bike—we learn in childhood, imitating others, and we wobble along until we can balance on two wheels without thinking about it.

Shy people often avoid social encounters with others, letting what social skills they have languish, or letting their anxiety absorb so much of their attention that they have none left over for prac-ticing the art of friendliness. This chapter invites you to pick up where you left off. You probably have more expertise than you realize. Even if you feel a little wobbly, with patience and practice you can build a repertoire of social graces that will eventually be-come second nature to you.

STUMBLING BLOCKS TO SOCIAL SKILLS

Have you ever been at a party and wondered why you bothered to make the effort of attending? Perhaps you're hovering on the edge of a group of people carrying on a conversation when a friend says to you, "You don't look like you're having a very good time." You mumble something about being "fine" and "enjoying yourself."

But you're not. Every time you interject a comment into the conversation you shake, you can't think of anything funny or interesting to talk about, and you wish you'd worn your jeans instead of your tweed pants.

The real problem is you *are* doing fine—only you don't recognize it. Dozens of studies confirm that shy people consistently give themselves much lower ratings for their social skills than do objective observers.[1] While observers do see some lack of social skills in shy people, most of you underestimate how well you're doing.

The mirror that so distorts your view of your own behavior is the self-absorption trap. You're so critical of yourself that you miss the conversation. The normal flow of positive feedback—which would give you an accurate picture of how things are proceeding—can't penetrate your screen of negative mental chatter. You're wasting the social skills you do have, *and you're not seeing yourself as others do.*

When you walk into a social situation telling yourself that you're bound to make a fool of yourself and that, as a result, others won't like you, you're not giving yourself a chance. By anticipating rejection, you invite it. You mentally tie yourself up in knots, you forget to express interest in others, your end of the conversation falters—and people conclude you don't like *them!*

Before you can improve your social skills, you've got to improve your self-image, fight back your irrational beliefs, and stop your negative self-talk. Maintaining a negative stance supports a defensive position. You're ready to reject others before they can reject you. If you skipped the exercises in Chapters 3 and 4, now is the time to go back and look at them—you can't gain social confidence if you're concentrating on what a slug you are, or if you are terribly self-conscious.

WHERE DO YOU GO WRONG?

Reading through the research on shy people's interactions, I compiled a list of ways that their social behavior differs from that of more confident people.

Compared to the socially self-confident, shy people . . .

- initiate fewer conversations, passively waiting to respond to others
- talk less, smile less, and make less eye contact
- show fewer facial expressions
- rely on "back-channel" responses (yes, uh-huh), designed to keep the other person talking instead of taking their own turn speaking
- reveal less personal information about themselves
- avoid arguments
- are reluctant to express strong personal opinions
- conform to the majority opinion in a group setting
- make less use of objective information statements, questions, acknowledgments, and confirmations
- stand farther away from their conversational partner

Behaving this way adds up to a *defensive* strategy for coping with social situations.[2] How many of these did you recognize in yourself? Wouldn't you like to give them up and adopt an *active* strategy for handling social situations?

LEARNING SOCIAL SKILLS

The worst part about stepping into a social situation is your fear that you won't know what to do or say. Mastering social skills can increase your sense of personal control. As your confidence mounts, your fears diminish. You can depend on effective coping strategies to keep anxiety at bay.

You can't, however, improve your social skills by sitting home alone and thinking about it. You'll have to immerse yourself in the actual situations that make you feel uncomfortable in order to practice new social techniques, and to find out what works for you and what doesn't. That's the hard part—staring down your anxiety —but there are ways to ease into it gradually.

ON BEING ASSERTIVE

Before I tell you more about practicing social skills, I want to address the issue of assertiveness. In the last fifteen years, assertiveness training has been a hot topic, with classes and books urging people to develop a whole new way of relating.

Being assertive means being able to express what you want, need, or desire while at the same time considering the feelings of other people.[3] Aggression, often confused with assertiveness, is going after what you want, with whatever it takes, without considering the consequences on others.

Although assertiveness, infinitely preferable to aggressiveness, sounds like the ideal way of relating to the world, circumstances sometimes call for alternatives. Karen Horney, a psychiatrist and personality theorist, outlined three broad styles of social behavior: moving away from other people, moving toward them, and moving against them.[4] In Horney's view, our childhood experiences tend to make us prefer one of these styles over the others.

Shy people often adopt the behavioral style of moving away— avoiding people and situations that make them feel uncomfortable. Extroverts adopt a style of moving toward others—being open, friendly, and agreeable. Shy behavior can also be classified as "moving toward" if you go along with the crowd when you really rather wouldn't or hold your tongue rather than disagree. Assertiveness and aggression, both involving confrontation, are moving against others—seeking what you want.

The key to successful social behavior is creating a balance between these three styles, and being flexible. As appealing as assertiveness may be, it's not something to strive for in every situation. Learn how and when to seek what you want. Rather than automatically saying to yourself "I should be assertive," ask: "Is this an instance when I need to be assertive?"

For example, when someone cuts in line at the movie theater, that's an appropriate time to be assertive, *if you so choose*. You can say, "Excuse me, we've all been waiting in line a long time and would appreciate it if you'd wait your turn too at the end of the line." If it doesn't really matter to you, if you're not going to stew about the person cutting in line, then you can let the situation go by. You make the choice whether or not to be assertive.

Choosing to move away may be the appropriate choice in some circumstances. After a particularly harried week at work, there's nothing wrong with recharging your batteries at home, *alone*, watching TV, reading a novel, or puttering around the house. If you bump shoulders with a man on a crowded street who turns, steps toward you with balled fists, and fires off a string of profanities, it's critical to move away—fast.

The problem for most people is that they get stuck in one pattern of behavior—of always being shy (moving away) or always being confrontational (moving against), or always being a "yes man" (moving toward). Shy people face a struggle every time they need to put their own interests first, so the mistaken assumption that to be normal means being assertive in every situation is overwhelming—a golden ring, always out of reach. The truth is that you don't need to be assertive in every situation. Strive for a balance, focusing on applying the behavior that best fits the situation.

WATCHING THE EXPERTS

You already started learning social skills when you practiced decentering in Chapter 4. The goal of that exercise was to keep your attention focused on others instead of on yourself. You can now add another dimension to decentering, picking up behavioral tips from what you see.

Modeling: As a small child you learned a whole complex of behaviors just by observing other people. For example, you learned that people shake hands when meeting a new person, when greeting someone familiar, and when taking leave of both new and old acquaintances. Embraces or kisses are reserved for close relatives or friends, with certain exceptions, such as at important celebrations or reunions after long absences.

Watching and imitating other people is one of the best ways to pick up the skills you missed at an earlier age. At this stage of the game, you don't have to change your behavior, but you *will* have to brave your anxieties to get yourself into the social situations that you need to observe. Anytime your anxious thoughts and worries assert themselves, remember to combat them with the exercises in Chapters 3 and 4.

In your self-development notebook begin a log of the social skills you observe. Whenever a setting makes you feel uncomfortable, practice decentering. Your goal is to watch how other people handle themselves. What are they doing and saying? In your notebook, briefly describe the setting and then list the social skills you observed. (Sometimes it will help to give little descriptions of the people you observed to joggle your memory on their approaches to a social encounter.) Which ones did you like? Which ones were not your style? Which behaviors were effective? Which weren't?

Here's an example of how your log might look:

SITUATION: GETTING HELP FROM A DEPARTMENT STORE SALES CLERK

Lady in red coat yelled loudly, "Oh, miss! Oh, miss! I need some help here. Do you want to make a sale or not? What does it take to get some assistance around here?"

COMMENT: Too rude. Saleswoman looked annoyed.

Man with hat on let someone else get ahead of him because he didn't speak up loudly enough; he only mumbled, "I'd like some help selecting a watch." He finally left without ever talking to the salesperson.

COMMENT: He should have told the person who pushed his way to the counter that he was there first.

Young woman in blue jeans smiled at sales clerk and asked politely for help. Said something like, "I want to buy a watch for my boyfriend's birthday.

Could you show me what you have in a moderate price range?" Sales clerk smiled right back at her and immediately gave her his full attention.
COMMENT: Good approach.

Don't use modeling to become a clone of someone else. You're looking for adaptable techniques that elicit the best response, whether you're at a party, shopping, working with new employees, or at any other social encounter. Adapt the behaviors you like, and avoid imitating the ineffective or unpleasant behaviors you observe (one afternoon at a store's complaint desk will demonstrate that pushiness is not always the best policy). You'll see that some people are more socially skilled than others, but that even those with unpolished skills still function quite happily in the social world.

Remember to set your goals. You'll find yourself in more social situations each day than you have time to record. You could make it your goal to log in one social observation each day, or at least four times a week, or whatever suits your time and energy level.

POSITIVE IMAGERY: After you've observed and recorded a half-dozen social techniques, you can begin using positive imagery, mentally practicing the behaviors you'd like to acquire.

Relax and imagine you're in one of your shyness situations. Now picture how you're going to act in that situation. See yourself calm and relaxed, applying a technique you've learned about from your observations. How are you acting? What are you saying? How do you look? How are the other people in your scene responding to you? Imagine your social encounter in as much detail as possible, and be sure to imagine it having a happy ending.

You're accomplishing two things in this exercise. First, you're mentally rehearsing the new behaviors you want to adopt. Second, you're programming yourself for *positive* action. Instead of worrying that you don't know what to do, you're learning and practicing what to do.

DRESS REHEARSAL: You don't want to live your social life in your imagination forever, so it's time for dress rehearsals. Don't panic—you're still within the safety of your own home.

If you have a trusted friend or relative whose help you can enlist, I think you'll find your dress rehearsals easier. Tell this person that you often feel uncomfortable in social situations and that you're practicing social skills so that you won't have to be nervous anymore. Ask if he or she would be willing to role-play and coach you during your practice sessions.

If you feel reluctant to confide in someone, you can always practice in front of a mirror by yourself. But I would like to encourage you to enlist the help of another person. Research shows that this type of practice helps the transition into real-life encounters, and the addition of a helper can make a significant difference.[5] Your confidant can lend support and encouragement, add his or her own tips for handling social situations, and give you the positive reinforcement you need to keep you working toward your goals.

If you've never participated in role-playing before, it can take a little while to get yourself into it. Many people feel embarrassed and giggly when they first try role-playing, and that's okay. Just keep working at it until you can take on roles without feeling self-conscious.

Choose a situation from your shyness list. Start with something small and well-defined, like the department store example I gave. Think about what new social skills you'd like to apply to this situation. Describe the situation and setting to your friend, along with what particular skills or effect you're practicing, and what role you'd like the other person to play. You, of course, play yourself with your newly acquired social repertoire.

You may master your new role quite quickly, or it may take several sessions until you feel self-confident. However long it takes, keep rehearsing until you feel sure of yourself. Ask your friend for feedback. And remember to *accept* positive feedback.

THE REAL WORLD

You can do it. You've been practicing at home, but now you've got to get out there in the real world and exercise your new skills.

Before you enter your first *real* shyness situation, take a few minutes beforehand to visualize yourself sailing through it just as you've practiced. If you have physical symptoms of anxiety, remember to make use of the relaxation techniques you learned in Chapter 2. And then go to it. You've been through it a hundred times in your imagination and you've practiced it repeatedly at home. Walk into that situation knowing that you know just what to do.

Don't get flustered if the unsuspecting players in this real-life drama don't stick to their lines. (After all, they don't know what their lines are supposed to be!) Maybe your mind suddenly goes blank. Maybe you can't bring yourself to say and do the things you've been practicing. It didn't go like you'd planned. Perhaps you tried a situation like the one in the department store described earlier and you encountered a rude salesperson. It isn't your fault you chanced upon someone who isn't willing to be helpful. If you begin to lose your nerve, don't slip into negativity—use positive self-talk until you're calm again. Then pick up where you left off before your anxiety got the better of you.

There's always a tendency to become discouraged when making the transition from practicing at home to the real world, especially after a poor encounter. Don't give up. Go back to role-playing until you're comfortable, and when you're ready, try your situation again. Keep practicing your situation over and over again in the real world until you're at ease with it. Remember, though, that real life is never perfectly predictable and daily encounters with strangers will always be more challenging (and exciting!) than role-playing.

Working up through your shyness list, repeat each of these steps:

- modeling
- visualizing
- role-playing
- real-life practice

Using this approach, you treat each shyness situation as a fresh project, moving into more difficult situations as your confidence increases.

Thus far, I've outlined the broadest techniques, methods that apply to all social situations. But you'll also want to practice the small details in each social picture. As you read the following sections, you'll probably recognize some of them from your own observations. Look for these finer details in the situations you observe, and incorporate them into your modeling, visualizing, and role-playing.

THE FINE ART OF CONVERSATION

There are three attitudes that influence communication: your attitude toward yourself, your attitude toward others, and your attitude toward communication itself.

I've already talked about your attitude toward yourself in Chapter 3—improving your self-esteem. And I've also talked about your attitude toward others, learning not to assume that other people are going to reject you automatically. Now let's look at what some of your attitudes may be toward communication.

Gerald M. Phillips, a speech communication professor at Pennsylvania State University, studies *rhetoritherapy* (teaching speech skills in everyday situations).[6] He's found that shy people often have assumptions about speech that serve as *excuses* for remaining silent:

- Talkative people were born that way, not made.
- Learning the pointers of good conversation is really learning how to manipulate others.
- Most people talk too much, and small talk is an especially silly waste of time.
- I'm a good listener and, after all, somebody has to listen since everyone else is talking.

Let's question each assumption. Are talkative people "born that way"? Not at all. Just as you've learned that your shyness was shaped and reinforced, whether or not you were born with the shy temperament, the loquacious among us also learned their style of relating. They weren't born talking a mile a minute. As your response to some situations is to clam up, some people chatter away nervously instead.

It's *not* manipulation to learn how to make others feel comfortable in social settings. Showing interest in others and drawing them out gives you a chance to get to know them, and for them to get to know you. In the process everyone feels valued.

Small talk is the bête noire of shy people. In Stephen Sondheim's play *Company,* one of the characters bemoans his inability to make "tea noises," the polite, seemingly trivial chatter that passes among strangers at parties. President Franklin Roosevelt, who found the small talk at White House functions mind-numbingly tedious, complained that people rarely listened to each other. To amuse himself—and prove a point—he often opened his conversation with the line, "I murdered my mother this morning." Astonishingly, most people nodded approvingly. (One astute listener shot back: "I'm sure she had it coming to her.")

Nevertheless, small talk serves a useful purpose. It allows people to comfortably warm up to one another. You can find out if you share common interests, and what brings the other person to the situation you're both in. In short, you'll find topics for lengthier conversation through the tidbits you pick up during small talk. Think of small talk as the appetizer before the main-course conversation.

Regarding the last of Phillips's assumptions, everyone agrees that being a good listener is an admirable quality. But are you really listening or are you focusing on your own thoughts and worries and merely giving the appearance of listening? How will people know you're listening if you don't occasionally give some response to what you're hearing?

I hope that these arguments dispel any resistance you might have about learning the art of conversation. Learning conversational skills isn't silly or manipulative or a waste of time—it's a more productive use of your mental energies.

To start off, let's look at the two broad components of conversation, self-disclosure and empathic listening.

SELF-DISCLOSURE

All of us have had the experience of standing alone in a roomful of merrily chatting strangers, wondering what the devil they're talking about. It's quite simple: They're talking about themselves. A hefty part of conversation is made up of self-disclosure. In new relationships, self-disclosure unfolds gradually, a tactful dance of veils in which each person reveals more and more about his personal life, thoughts, and opinions. Usually, the partners offer bits and pieces of themselves at the same pace, each revealing about the same amount of information as the other. But there are some exceptions to this general rule.

One is when two strangers have encountered one another and the chances of meeting again are slim. In this case, the two will often reveal a great deal about themselves. It's easier to tell a secret about yourself to a stranger you won't ever see again than it is to expose yourself to someone you expect to see in the future. With strangers you aren't left in the awkward position of seeing them again and realizing that they know more about you than you know about them.

Another exception occurs between close friends. When a good friend comes to you with a personal problem, you're expected to listen sympathetically and perhaps offer advice. You're not expected to respond with an equally intimate account of one of your own problems. Because the friendship is already based on trust and reciprocity, your friend knows that when the time comes you'll probably entrust him or her with one of your problems.[7]

Self-disclosure may seem a little tricky at first. You have to listen to the content of the other person's conversation. How much is he or she revealing? How well do you already know the person? What is your relationship? Is it appropriate for you to reveal as much?

There's nothing quite so disconcerting as having someone you barely know walk up to you and immediately launch into a long monologue about his or her tragic childhood or rotten marriage. While they're spilling their guts, you're left wondering if you were just a random target for hearing all this very personal information. You feel uncomfortable because you have no idea what to say to this person you don't even know.

In most cases, self-disclosure should be a slow process, and there are ways you can use self-disclosure to gradually open up to others during conversation.

• *Give more than the facts.* When discussing a book, a news story, a movie, or a TV program, let your listeners know your opinion, let them see a little bit of you behind the facts of a story. If you read in the newspaper that one person won the largest jackpot ever in your state's lottery, don't just exclaim over the dollar amount. Tell your friend what lifelong ambitions you could realize if you had that money at *your* disposal.

• *Describe yourself in a situation.* If someone asks you how your autumn trip to the White Mountains went, don't just tell what you did and saw on your trip. Describe yourself in the situation. "There I was trying to find my way in the dark to the latrine when I walked into this big furry thing. I froze in my tracks—my imagination went wild—I thought I'd walked right into a bear! I felt so silly when it turned out to be a fellow camper with his wife's rabbit-skin jacket on trying to find his way back from the latrine!"

• *Give a balanced picture of yourself.* None of us is perfect, and people don't enjoy conversing with someone who only talks about their positive qualities and experiences. Such a person doesn't seem genuine. We wonder if they're conceited or just lucky to have a perfect life. Small admissions of faults or even politely disagreeing with someone makes us seem more human and real to other people. For example, "Guess what? I got my promotion! I didn't realize until now that being a manager is more difficult than it looks."

Remember when talking about yourself to take into account who you're talking with. How well do you know the other person?

Where you are—are you in circumstances where a very personal conversation is appropriate or inappropriate? How much is the other person disclosing?

If you're unaccustomed to revealing much about yourself, it might take a little while to get the balance right. If you go overboard with self-disclosure, people will be put off knowing too much about you too soon. If you refuse to open up to others, you'll seem cold and unfriendly.[8] You won't be able to form fast friendships if the other person isn't allowed to learn what your interests are, what motivates you, what kind of person you are.

One way to gauge how much to disclose about yourself is by thinking about how much you'd like to know about the other person. What kinds of things could someone you've just met tell you that you'd find interesting but not uncomfortable? Someone you've known for a long time? Someone who's a new friend?

EMPATHIC LISTENING

Self-disclosure rounds out conversational topics and at the same time allows people to get to know you. When it's time to respond, there's another skill you can learn that will come in handy: empathic listening. You'll find it much easier to keep a conversation going if you spend your listening time concentrating on the other person instead of thinking about what you're going to say when it's your turn to speak next.

Empathic listening is identical to decentering. You focus on the other person, not on yourself. As you listen, imagine yourself in the speaker's shoes. How would you feel after being in the situation they just told you about? What kind of feelings do you think lie behind the opinion they just expressed? What would you like someone to say to you if you'd just told a sad story? Or a happy story?

With empathic listening and responding you won't have to worry about what to say because conversation will naturally surface when you've given your attention to what was said and imagining how the other person feels.

BASIC CONVERSATION 101

There are many other finer details of conversation beyond the larger areas of self-disclosure and empathic listening. Let's look at some of these now. You're not going to believe this, but you don't have to say anything particularly clever in order to start a conversation with a stranger. All you're doing is breaking the ice, giving the other person an opportunity to chat with you.

Here are a number of ways to approach someone you think you'd like to talk to:[9]

• *Introduce yourself.* Simply walk up to someone and introduce yourself. For example, a friend of mine always used to see the same man at her bus stop each morning. They occasionally nodded at one another, but never spoke. Finally, one morning she arrived at the bus stop, looked him in the eye, smiled, and said, "Hi, I'm Nicole. I see you here every day. It looks like it's gonna be great weather today, doesn't it?" There was nothing catchy or clever about Nicole's approach, but it broke the ice. Until Tom, her bus-stop companion, moved to a different part of town, they each enjoyed passing the time waiting for the bus talking together.

• *Ask a question.* When you find yourself in an unfamiliar place or situation, you can always try opening a conversation by asking a question. You can ask someone, "Does this restaurant always have a waiting list at lunchtime?" or "I just moved here—what's especially fun to do in this town?" Let your natural curiosity bubble to the surface and you'll find that other people are often only too happy to answer your questions.

• *Give a compliment.* Don't give a compliment you don't mean. Other people will see through you right away. But, when you truly admire an article of clothing or a possession, go ahead and open a conversation that way. For example: "I love your shoes. I've been looking for a pair that has low heels like yours. Where did you get them?" or "That's a funny bumper sticker you have on your car. Where did you find it?" Following up your compliment with a question gives the other person the opportunity to keep the conversation going after saying "Thank you."

• *A surefire tip: Smile!* Most people can't resist a genuine smile —it's powerful and disarming. Try it. With any luck, they'll walk right up and say hello.

KEEPING THINGS GOING

After you've started a conversation, you'll need to expend some effort to keep it going. The way to do that is by responding empathically. Here are a few tips:[10]

• *Ask open-ended questions.* If you ask someone "Do you like living here?" you're bound to get a yes or no for an answer. Instead ask: "What do you like about living here?" Open-ended questions allow people to expand on their answers. Anytime you ask a question that can be answered with a very brief reply the conversation comes perilously close to being short-lived. Use *why* and *how* questions to draw out your conversational partners and you'll find that their answers give you more than enough information you can use to continue the conversation.

• *Talk about the situation.* You can use your surroundings as a conversational topic. Make a statement about the situation you find yourself in and your feelings about it. "It's so noisy in this bar, I can hardly hear myself think!" Or: "On rainy days like these I always want to curl up with a good book instead of going to work."

• *Use questions and answers.* When people ask you close-ended questions, try to give open-ended answers. In your mind rephrase their close-ended question into an open-ended question and then reply. Next, toss the conversational ball back to them by following your answer with a question. "Yes, I enjoy the museums, theaters, and street life of this city. There's always something to do. Are you new in town?"

• *Follow through.* Use the information you hear to follow up. For example, if someone says, "I've only just started reading the Clancy book . . . I usually read mystery novels," you can exclaim that mystery novels are also your passion and exchange views on various mystery authors or indicate your interest in knowing the person's opinion as to who the best mystery writers are.

HANDLING COMPLIMENTS.   We love and hate to get compliments. They make us feel appreciated and good about ourselves, but many of us don't know how to respond to a compliment. For shy people who are battling to keep up a positive self-image, compliments are often received with less than graceful aplomb.

You may be complimented on any number of things: your performance for a job well done, your appearance, some aspect of your personality, or a prized possession. The compliments that mean the most are the ones we receive about our personality.

You might think that a simple "thank you" conveys some kind of conceitedness, as if you already know and expect compliments on your new suit or beguiling smile. Not so. A simple "thank you" is the least you can do to respond to a compliment. If you reply to a compliment with embarrassment, you might make the giver feel awkward for obviously making you feel uncomfortable, though that wasn't their intention. If you say "thank you" and then add a disclaimer ("it's an old dress"), you diminish the gift intended by the compliment. And to make no response at all to a compliment is rude.

If you're flustered by a compliment, at least say "thank you." Better yet, add a little something to your reply: "Oh, thank you. I worked extra hard on this project and I feel very satisfied with the results." Or: "How nice of you to say so. I hunted through zillions of stores and thought I'd never find the perfect scarf to match this coat."

WHEN CONVERSATION FAILS

What if you approach someone for conversation and he or she is unresponsive? What does it mean? It *doesn't* mean you're unlikable. There are any number of reasons why an attempted conversation fails. It could be that the other person doesn't feel like talking at that moment, or is preoccupied with other thoughts, or maybe even shy! When you run into someone who doesn't respond to your conversational opener, don't take it personally. Brush it off, move on to the next person, and try again.

THE BALANCE OF CONVERSATION

Talking and listening per se don't add up to a rewarding exchange between people. Listener and speaker need to balance and alternate their roles. If someone talks nonstop, we resent being unable to get a word in edgewise. If someone remains quiet, we may feel that we have to do more than our share to keep conversation flowing and therefore conclude that the other person isn't really interested in us or the conversation.

Chris Kleinke, a psychologist at the University of Alaska, and his colleagues conducted a study to find the optimal balance of conversation.[11] Participants listened to three different recorded conversations. Each conversation had two speakers, one female and one male, and was balanced differently. Kleinke asked his participants to rate each of the couples for likableness (participants didn't know that the researchers were actually interested in the balance of conversation).

CONVERSATION 1: Man speaks for eighty percent of the time
Woman speaks for twenty percent of the time

CONVERSATION 2: Man speaks for twenty percent of the time
Woman speaks for eighty percent of the time

CONVERSATION 3: Man speaks for fifty percent of the time
Woman speaks for fifty percent of the time

Kleinke found that his participants most liked the couple who shared the conversational time equally; those who spoke for only twenty percent of the time were perceived as very introverted. And, shy women take note: While Kleinke expected that his participants would like the man who dominated the conversational time better than the woman who did, this was *not* the case. Kleinke's study demonstrates that people expect us to hold up our end of the conversation, no matter what our gender is. Listening intently with a sympathetic look on your face isn't enough to show your partner that you're indeed hearing and responding to what they're saying. A satisfying exchange relies on equal participation by both people.

BODY LANGUAGE

Although our voices carry the words of our conversation, our bodies also speak volumes to our listeners.[12] Becoming aware of your gestures, body orientation, and eye contact can help you become a more effective communicator. Many of us are expert interpreters of body language without even being aware of it. Gestures, eye contact, touching, and interpersonal distance are all learned behaviors and vary from culture to culture. You can use body language to send intended messages—for example, to make yourself appear approachable.

If you were to study a videotape of your own nonverbal behavior, you might see what I did when I studied the body language of shy people. Almost every shy person sat as far away as possible from their conversational partner, avoided direct eye contact, shifted their body away from the other person, and fidgeted. The nonverbal messages were "I'm not open to speaking with you" and "You make me nervous."

• *Personal space:* Psychologists have determined approximate interpersonal distances for various types of relationships.[13] People who are intimate with one another maintain a distance of zero to eighteen inches between themselves. Intimate distance is usually reserved for private time, but a crowded subway would be an exception to this rule. In public, personal distance usually varies from one-and-a-half feet to four feet, depending upon the relationship between the people. Typical social distance ranges from four to twelve feet, again depending on the people and circumstances of the situation.

If you stand too far away from people, they may think you're unfriendly or don't want to talk to them. Since you can't walk around with a ruler measuring out just the right distance, you'll need to watch the distances that people keep between themselves when talking. You probably stand or sit too far away from them, so move in a little closer. If another person backs away a little bit, then you'll know you've come in too close.

• *Eye contact:* When we begin speaking, we almost immediately look away after the first word or two is out of our mouths. If we're talking for a while, we check back with our eyes occasionally to see how our listener is responding. Meanwhile, the listener keeps a fairly steady gaze on us while we speak. When we know we're coming to the end of our talk, we look directly at our listener for the last few moments while still speaking. This is the cue to the listener that we're just about finished speaking and it's his turn to respond.

When the normal pattern of eye contact is broken, unintended messages may be sent. Shy people tend to avoid looking at their conversational partners because they're feeling anxious. Unfortunately, this is frequently interpreted as boredom or aloofness by the other person. Imagine if someone is listening to you speak and all the while gazing around the room. You'd think, "This person is bored with what I'm saying and can't wait to get away." And if you ignore the eye contact that says "Okay, now it's your turn to speak," awkward silences may follow or the other person may politely keep the conversation going, but wonder why you're not responding or holding up your end of the exchange.

Watch the eye contact between people who are talking and you'll see the pattern quite clearly. You don't want to stare at another person, because that's taken as a sign of aggression or hostility. But try to give other people more eye contact and you'll find that communication becomes friendlier and more open.

• *Body orientation:* You don't have to sit or stand nose-to-nose with someone else—in fact, it's quite common for two people to stand with their shoulders angled slightly out—but you don't want to wrap yourself up tightly or angle yourself too far away from another person. If you sit with your legs crossed, your arms crossed, and your shoulders turned away from your partner, you send a message that you're not open to conversation. This is just the way many of the shy people in my videotape study sat.

Watch how other people position their bodies when they're talking and keep a careful watch on your own body orientation to make sure that you're not sending out the wrong message. An old interviewer's trick to show interest in another person is to lean forward slightly while that person is speaking.

• *Nervous gestures:* Sometimes it's hard to know what to do with our hands when we're talking. Many people use their hands expressively—we've all seen people who seem to talk as much with their hands as with their mouths. Shy people, however, tend to fidget with their hands, nervously pulling at their hair and tugging at their clothing. Like pencil- or finger-tapping, this is bound to make the other person feel nervous too. If nothing else will help, put your hands in your pockets or clasp them together to stop yourself from fidgeting.

Monitor your body language as much as you can without letting it become the entire focus of your interaction; you don't want to add to your self-consciousness. You may find it easier to work on one small negative habit at a time, rather than trying to coordinate every aspect of your body language at once.

COMING TO A CLOSE

It's not unusual to feel awkward about ending a conversation, either to leave a gathering or to move on to a new conversational partner.

End a conversation simply by telling the other person that you must leave because you have someplace else to go. If you've enjoyed the conversation, tell the person so: "I'm sorry I must leave now, I've got an appointment in a few minutes. I very much enjoyed talking with you." Or, at a cocktail party: "It's been very interesting chatting with you. I'm feeling hungry now, so I think I'll go see what munchies are on the buffet table."

If you'd like to see the other person again, end your conversation by saying how much you've liked talking to her and that you hope you'll see her again. If you talked about a common interest, informally suggest a meeting and see whether the interest is mutual. "So long, it's been nice talking with you. We should get together sometime and have a game of racquetball."

Now that you've discovered your type of shyness and begun taking steps to overcome it, it's time to apply your improving social skills and confidence to the important life areas of friendship, romance, and career.

APPLYING YOUR NEW CONFIDENCE TO YOUR SOCIAL LIFE

CHAPTER 6

Writing Scripts

It's hard to think of actress Kim Basinger as having been a shy teenager—she wanted to be a cheerleader, but froze during try-outs. Morgan Fairchild, who as a child worried about baby fat and the fact that she wore glasses, was so shy she used to become ill during acting classes. Sherman Hemsley, the irascible George Jefferson on the TV sitcom *The Jeffersons,* is quiet as a clam offstage.

Does the actor make the person or the person make the actor? The entertainment industry is rife with success stories of men and women who first stepped on stage, performed in front of a camera, or spoke into a microphone as a way of overcoming shyness. Orson Welles, Barbara Walters, Michael Caine, Henry Winkler, and Carol Burnett are just a few of the dozens of celebrities who have publicly confessed to shyness.[1] Entertainers learn early the advantages of playing roles, as Valerie Kaprisky, Richard Gere's sensuous costar in *Breathless,* explains: "When I was going to acting school, I was so shy. I couldn't do anything without feeling ridiculous. I broke out of it when I understood that once I was on stage or in front of the camera I could do anything, because it wasn't me. I had the alibi of the part."[2]

You, too, can use the alibi of a "part" to break out of your shyness. How? You enter your new role by practicing scripts that you write yourself. What happens when you don't *act* shy? You take on a new role as a non-shy person.

Scripts enable you to rehearse brief, but difficult, situations (from introducing yourself at a party to disagreeing with someone).[3] Obviously, this method has its limitations—you could hardly write a script for all the encounters you might have at a party—but you can use scripts to get you *started* in just about any situation and use the social-skills tips from Chapter 5 to keep you going.

WRITING AND PRACTICING YOUR SCRIPTS

First, decide what role you're playing: friendly party-goer, assertive medical patient, inquisitive student, information seeker, whatever. Imagine that it's a close friend who's asking for your advice. What would you tell him or her to say in a particular situation? In removing yourself from a situation, you're likely to find that your ideas flow freely and with less interruption from the anticipation of playing the part. If you like, you can write several different scripts for one situation, with your replies to a variety of possible responses.

Sample scripts for different situations follow below. After each sample, I'll ask you to write a script for a similar circumstance from the list of shyness situations you composed in Chapter 1. I can't possibly write out scripts for every situation that triggers your particular shyness, and even if I could, I wouldn't. My samples give you one person's idea of the tone (my own), but the words and expressions in your scripts should reflect *your* personality.

After you've written a script for one of your shyness situations, practice it with gusto. Mentally take on your role, and then repeat your lines out loud until you've memorized them. If you can get someone else to play the part of the fellow party-goer, doctor, professor, or information provider, so much the better. Like an actor rehearsing lines, you will find it's much easier when you've got a partner to work with.

When you feel comfortable with your script, try it out in your shyness situation. Pick up the phone and make that call to set up a dental appointment or request a household repair from your landlord. Try your friendly-introduction script at a party. Just remember: You're the only one who knows all the lines. Whereas actors have a safety net—*everyone* knows their lines—your scripts are more improvisational. Rarely will others respond exactly as you've imagined. But don't let an unexpected response throw you off balance; instead improvise the next line.

INTRODUCING YOURSELF

One of the most difficult social situations shy people encounter is introducing themselves to a stranger. Whether you're meeting a new employee at the office or mingling at a party, the simple act of exchanging names becomes a very scary prospect.

When you're introducing yourself, your mind may become filled with a stream of silent reminders: smile, shake hands, say your name, think of something to say after your name. With all that chatter going on in your head, it's no wonder you never hear the name of your new acquaintance!

An old and useful tip for remembering the name of someone you've just met is to immediately repeat his or her name out loud. The easiest thing to say next is a remark on the situation you both find yourself in.

SETTING: Monthly meeting for your division at work. While sipping coffee before the meeting, you see a man you've recently noticed a lot in the hallways on your trips to the copy room. You walk over to him . . .

YOU: Hello, I'm Jessica. I've passed you in the hallways quite a bit recently and thought I'd introduce myself.

HE: Hi, it's nice to meet you! I'm Nathan.

YOU: It's good to meet you, Nathan. Did you just start with the company or did you transfer from our California office?

HE: No, I'm brand-new—just started about three weeks ago. This is my first division meeting. What's the usual agenda for these meetings?

YOU: Well, first Mr. Driscoll reports on our division's performance for the last month, and then outlines this month's plans and tells us about any new company policies. After that . . .

Is there somebody new in your environment that you've been wanting to meet? How would you approach that person? In your self-development notebook, write out a script including a brief description of the setting where you'd be likely to have the opportunity to introduce yourself.

_____
_____
_____
_____
_____
_____
_____

Have you ever bumped into someone and recognized the face, but couldn't recall the name? Don't feel embarrassed—it happens to everyone. The best approach is to remind the person where the two of you met, and reintroduce yourself in case they can't remember your name either!

SETTING: On a Saturday shopping expedition, you see a man browsing in the next aisle at the bookstore. You rack your brain to remember his name, but it's no use. He glances your way and seems to recognize you. You walk over to him . . .

YOU: Hi, I believe we met some time ago at the county book auction. I'm Paul.

HE: Oh, Paul, I thought I knew your face but I couldn't remember where I'd met you before. I'm Alan.

YOU: It's good to see you again, Alan. Are you hunting down a particular book today or just browsing?

HE: I'm just browsing today to see what new books are out. Listen, I saw a notice in the paper the other day for a book auction over in Hillsdale. Would you be interested in going with me? It's on the 25th.

YOU: That sounds great. Do you have time for a cup of coffee now and you could fill me in on the details?

The above script could use a "Plan B." Most of the time when you say your name, the other person will say theirs too. But what if they don't?

HE: Oh, Paul, I thought I knew your face but I couldn't remember where I'd met you before. How are you?

YOU: I'm fine, thanks, but I'm afraid I can't recall your name.

HE: I'm sorry, it's Alan.

What about a social situation in which you must introduce a friend to another friend or acquaintance? Introductions of this sort are fairly standard in form, though I think it's also helpful to tell each person how you know the other.

SETTING: On a break between classes you sit down in the college cafeteria for a cup of coffee. Kayla, whom you know from another class, joins you. Moments later a new acquaintance joins the two of you. It's time to introduce your two friends to one another . . .

YOU: Hi, Scott, I didn't know you had a break between classes now too. I'd like you to meet my friend Kayla. She's my History 210 study companion. Kayla, meet Scott. Scott and I suffer through French every day at the awful hour of 8:30 A.M.

KAYLA: Hi, Scott, nice to meet you. I took French last semester and it was a grind, I can tell you. You have all my sympathies.

SCOTT: Kayla, I can tell we feel the same way about this language requirement! Well, let's speak of pleasant things. Are either of you going to the basketball game on Friday night?

YOU: I'd like to, but I'm afraid I'll feel guilty if I don't spend the time boning up for midterms.

SCOTT: Oh, come on! Let's all three of us go. We can't spend *all* our time studying . . .

This is another script that calls for a "Plan B." Suppose you don't really know Scott all that well and you suddenly forget his name. A simple apology and a straightforward statement will serve you best.

YOU: Hi, I didn't know you had a break between classes now too. I'd like you to meet my friend Kayla—she's also my History 210 study companion. And now I feel positively awful because I can't remember your name!

SCOTT: Oh, don't worry about that—I'm terrible with names too. It's Scott.

YOU: Well, we're all set now. Scott, this is Kayla. Scott and I suffer through French every day at the awful hour of 8:30 A.M.

Try writing out a few scripts in your self-development notebook for introducing yourself and others. And when you're out there practicing it for real, remember to use your new skills from Chapter 5: asking open-ended questions, self-disclosing, choosing conversational topics from the situation you're in and using empathic listening and responding.

INFORMATION, PLEASE

Airline and hotel reservations, tourist information, class or seminar information, movie times, telephone numbers . . . Our lives depend on an endless amount of information—and we often get that information from people. Sometimes the person is an anonymous voice over the phone—a telephone operator or an administrator. At other times you'll be face-to-face with the person who can help you find out what you want to know—a librarian or a sales clerk.

Whether you're asking for information over the phone or in person, start with a short statement about the information you're seeking and ask if you're speaking with the correct person to get that information. If you begin with a long, complex story, you're unlikely to get the chance to finish before your call is transferred three or four times and you find yourself repeating the beginning of your story over and over again. When I make any call, I always write an abbreviated script. I include everything I need to find out so that I won't forget any important questions.

SETTING: For weeks you've been scanning the classified section of your newspaper, hoping to find someone who wants to sell an antique piano bench. At last you're rewarded with an ad that describes the very thing. You pick up the phone . . .

YOU: Hello, I'm calling about the ad in the *Guardian* for the piano bench. Are you the person I should speak to about it?

MAN: No, it's my wife who's selling it. Hold on for just a moment while I get her.

WOMAN: Hello.

YOU: Hi, I'm interested in the piano bench you've advertised for sale. May I ask you a few questions about it?

WOMAN: Oh, yes. What would you like to know?

YOU: What kind of wood is the bench made of, and does it have a padded seat? Also, is it in good condition and how much are you asking for it?

If "calling people I don't know" is one of the items on your shyness list, break down the task into smaller steps by writing your first script for the call that makes you feel the *least* shy. Practice it, try it out in a real-life situation, and then begin again with the next-most-difficult call to make. Remember: Take one step at a time on your road to overcoming shyness, and set realistic goals for yourself as you go along.

It's easy enough to write out a script for a telephone call, but approaching a research librarian (or worse, your boss) with a script in hand is a bit awkward. Write out the script for your face-to-face encounter, rehearse it, and then carry a "mini-script" with you, listing all the questions you need answered. Rather than thinking less of you for referring to a list of questions, people will probably be impressed with your professionalism.

SETTING: Your old car is fading away fast and you've decided to go car shopping. You're not sure whether you should buy a brand-new car or a used car that's only a few years old. You walk into a car dealership, and a salesman promptly appears at your side . . .

SALESMAN: Good afternoon, can I help you?

YOU: I'm only looking today, and I'm trying to get an idea of what a new car costs versus buying a reliable used car.

SALESMAN: I see. We have a good selection of used cars as well as new cars. I'm sure we'll be able to find something for you. How much do you want to spend?

YOU: Well, I'm not sure exactly. I'm looking for a car that gets good gas mileage and has low maintenance costs. Wait, I've got a list here of all my requirements. Let's see, oh, I almost forgot! I don't like driving a standard shift, so I'll want to get a car with automatic transmission. And I need to know about financing, whether your dealership has as good a rate as my bank does, and . . .

Look at your shyness-situations list and choose a face-to-face information-gathering situation that you've been avoiding. Remember to begin with the least fearful one, and don't be concerned about consulting your list of questions when you need to.

MAKING APPOINTMENTS

There are times when we must consult professionals for help, and making appointments with them can sometimes be intimidating. Doctors, dentists, lawyers, accountants, therapists—all are busy professionals who usually have an arsenal of buffers between them and you. When you call for an appointment you may get a secretary, an answering service, or an answering machine. Be prepared to leave your name and number and a preferred call-back time, and leave your script by the telephone so you can refer to it when your call is returned.

SETTING: You knew you should have made an appointment with the dentist earlier, and now your tooth is really aching, so you must make an emergency appointment . . .

RECEPTIONIST: Dr. Stevens's office.

YOU: Hello, this is Vanessa Smith and I'd like to make an appointment with Dr. Stevens as soon as possible.

RECEPTIONIST: Are you having trouble with a tooth?

YOU: Yes! One of my back molars is aching very badly.

RECEPTIONIST: Oh, dear. Have you seen Dr. Stevens before?

YOU: Yes, I have, but it's been a couple of years.

RECEPTIONIST: Okay, let me look in the book . . . I could fit you in today at 4:30 P.M. Would that be a good time for you?

YOU: That'll be fine. You can be sure this is one dental appointment I won't forget!

A more difficult call to work up the courage to make is one with a doctor when you need something more than a routine physical, or when you've decided you need professional help from a counselor for a problem in your life.

SETTING: You've left your name and number with the answering service for Dr. Evans, who is a therapist. A while later your phone rings . . .

YOU: Hello.

DR. EVANS: Hello, could I speak with Merrill Cox?

YOU: Speaking.

DR. EVANS: This is Dr. Evans returning your call.

YOU: Thank you for returning my call, Dr. Evans. You were recommended to me by my minister and I'm wondering if you are taking new clients at this time.

DR. EVANS: Yes, I am.

YOU: Could you also please tell me how long you've been in practice and what your orientation is?

DR. EVANS: I've been in practice for ten years, I'm a clinical psychologist, and I take a psychodynamic approach to therapy. Could you tell me briefly why you're seeking help?

YOU: I'm an extremely shy person and I've been working on overcoming it, but I feel that I need some outside help to really get over this thing. Have you worked much with other shy people?

DR. EVANS: I've worked with clients who are socially phobic, but I'm also familiar with the research literature on shyness.

YOU: Uh huh . . . What is your hourly fee?

DR. EVANS: My hourly fee is $75, and if you haven't already, you may want to see if your health insurance covers therapy.

YOU: Could we set up an initial consultation? Also, do you have evening appointments? I work during the day . . .

DR. EVANS: I'm afraid I don't have any evening hours available at this time, but I could see you early in the morning. Would you like to come in at 8 A.M. next Tuesday?

YOU: Yes, that would work out for me, I think. I need to get your address, and some directions.

When you need special help from a doctor or counselor, you feel vulnerable, and that's partially why these types of calls are hard for anyone to make. A script prepared in advance will enable you to make your call with greater confidence and poise.

THE VOICE OF AUTHORITY

It never fails. Whenever I'm driving and I see lights flashing in my rearview mirror, I immediately assume I've done something wrong. Inevitably, the police car flies past me in pursuit of something more dramatic than me driving five miles an hour over the speed limit. Nevertheless, it always takes a couple of minutes for my heart to slow down. There's something about authorities of any kind that pushes our panic buttons.

Whenever you're in the presence of an authority—a police officer, your supervisor, a teacher, a lawyer, a doctor—remember that they're people too. There's nothing magical or all-powerful about them. Authorities are people with special expertise who are trained to help you. You're only asking for what you need from them.

SETTING: You spent hours in the library working on your term paper and feel that you did a good job on it. When you get the paper back marked C+ you're shocked and unhappy. You decide to ask your professor why you got a lower grade than you felt you deserved . . .

YOU: Hello, Professor Casey. I'd like to talk with you about my grade on the term paper.

CASEY: I take it you're not happy with the grade?

YOU: No, I'm not. I worked very hard on this paper and I don't understand why I didn't get a better grade.

CASEY: I think I commented at the end of your paper that your coverage was incomplete. What you wrote was good, but your paper examines only one side of the topic. You chose an area that's extensive, and I think you may have lost sight of the balance. An "A" term paper would have discussed all sides of the issue.

YOU: But by the time I'd finished with the one area, my paper was already up to the maximum page length you set.

CASEY: Since this term paper counts fifty percent toward your final grade, I'll allow you to rewrite it. You'll need to cut the length on what you've written already and add a comprehensive discussion of the other areas.

YOU: I really appreciate that. I want to do well in your class, and I'd like to get a better grade on this paper.

Which "authorities" make your heart beat a little faster? Turn to your self-development notebook again and try writing out a few scripts for the ones you're reluctant to approach. Here's another example of speaking with an authority, one closer to home.

SETTING: You've just moved into a new apartment. The rent is affordable, and it's close to work. But the bathroom ceiling is chipped and peeling— the result of a leak that's been fixed. Although the ceiling isn't a hazard, it's an eyesore. You'd like to have it repaired . . .

YOU: Hi, Mr. Mahoney, this is Audrey Rowland, your new tenant in 5F. I'm calling to request a repair.

MAHONEY: What seems to be the problem?

YOU: I've just noticed that the bathroom ceiling is peeling. It looks like it's from an old leak. I'd really appreciate it if you could have it repaired.

MAHONEY: Is the ceiling damp?

YOU: No, I checked and it's quite dry.

MAHONEY: So this isn't an emergency repair . . .

YOU: No, it's not. But the ceiling is quite an eyesore, and I know you want to keep your property looking good. When would you be able to have the repair made?

MAHONEY: I'll come by tomorrow and have a look at it. I won't know till I see it if it's something I can do myself or if I'll have to call in a general contractor.

YOU: Thank you, Mr. Mahoney.

DIFFICULT EXCHANGES

Difficult exchanges are those when you want to be assertive without sounding demanding. In a conversation you might want to disagree with somebody's statement or opinion. In other circumstances you may need to ask for what you want, whether it's some time to yourself or seeing a different movie from the one suggested. Or perhaps a friend makes a request that you can't or don't want to oblige and you want to say "no."

Shy people are often reluctant to express their own opinion, especially when it's not the majority view. Here's an example of how to handle such a situation.

SETTING: During a backyard cookout you're talking with your neighbors. The topic of the new seat-belt law comes up and both your neighbors agree that the state shouldn't tell you whether or not you must wear a seat belt. You see it differently and have strong feelings about it . . .

BOB: Hey, did you hear that the new seat-belt law passed? It makes you wonder what we'll be told to do next!

JOSH: Yeah, I read about that in the newspaper this morning. It really burns me up. It should be my choice whether or not I wear my seat belt.

YOU: I have to disagree with you two. I think the seat-belt law is a good idea.

JOSH: How can you say that? Our lives are already too regulated by laws. I hurt only myself by not wearing a seat belt—it doesn't affect anyone else.

YOU: But every accident affects us all. When you send yourself flying through the windshield, the police are called, an ambulance is sent, and you end up in the emergency room. It costs taxpayers' dollars to clean up every accident, and our auto insurance rates go up to cover unnecessary injuries. If nothing else, you can look at the seat-belt law as an economic measure.

BOB: I see your point. I'm still not sure I like being told what to do, but I can see your side of the argument.

JOSH: I don't know. I guess I'll have to think about it some more.

Disagreeing with a majority opinion makes us stand out from the crowd. Research shows that for shy people, dissenting from the majority view is difficult.[4] If a topic comes up and you have strong feelings about it, it's sometimes better to put in your two cents than appear to agree by saying nothing at all. When you hide your true feelings, you make it difficult for other people to get to know the real you. Argue your view with facts, not personal accusations, and others won't feel attacked. They may even be persuaded to give your side of the issue serious reconsideration.

Group activities involve give-and-take. Sometimes you end up doing something that suits you perfectly and at other times you participate in an activity that's not your first choice. And then there are occasions when you don't want to go along with the proposed idea . . .

SETTING: Discussing with two of your friends what movie to see that evening, they both think it would be wonderful to scare themselves silly with a horror movie. You can't join in this enthusiasm because you hate such films . . .

FRIEND 1:   I know! *Psycho* is playing at the Orpheus, let's go to that. I haven't seen it in years.

FRIEND 2:   I've never seen *Psycho*. I've heard it's really chilling.

YOU: Oh, I really don't like horror movies.

FRIEND 2:   Come on, this is Hitchcock! It's a classic.

FRIEND 2: Yeah . . . besides, it's not like *Halloween, Part 20* or something like that. You've just got to see this movie.

YOU: Listen, I *like* to take showers, and I've heard about that scene! Let's try a thriller instead. How about *The Manchurian Candidate*? It's a great film and it's playing at the Biograph. You don't see it being revived very often.

FRIEND 1: Well, I guess I could go for a thriller.

FRIEND 2: Yeah, a thriller would be good. I'd be happy with that.

YOU: Great—you don't know how relieved I am. Let's see, it's playing at 7:30 and 9:40. Do we want to go to the early or late show?

It's hard for some of us to do, but saying "no" is a part of life. If you don't learn to say it, you'll end up doing things you don't want to do or overextending yourself in an effort to please everyone.

SETTING: A friend at work asks you if you'll read his monthly report before he gives it to the boss on Monday. It's Friday afternoon, you've had an unusually busy week at work, and your weekend is already full. There'll scarcely be time for you to relax, let alone sit down for a few hours to critique his report . . .

WALTER: Hi! Look, I've just finished my first monthly report, but I'm feeling anxious about it and I wondered if you'd mind taking it home with you over the weekend and letting me know what you think.

YOU: Gee, Walter, my weekend is pretty full as it is. It's one of those weekends when there's something planned for every minute.

WALTER: Oh. Well, it's just that you've done lots of these reports before and this is my first one and I really want to make a good impression on the boss.

YOU: Walter, I can't imagine you turning in any work that's less than superb! I could glance at it quickly for you now, but I'm sorry I can't give you more time with it than that. It doesn't happen very often, but this time my weekend is booked solid.

WALTER: I understand. Well, if you could just give it a once-over that would make me feel better.

When you encounter someone who is very persistent, who tries to wear you down to saying "yes," you have but one alternative. You repeat yourself, playing your message like a broken record until it finally sinks in. If you can't bring yourself to refuse a request directly, tell the other person you'll think about it, that you'll have to check your calendar first, and that you'll get back to her later with an answer. Then rehearse the good reasons you have for saying "no" and be sure you do get back with an answer.

To sum up: Scripts can help you practice what to say in a variety of situations, and stepping into a role can help you chase away shy feelings. Look at the Italian actor Giancarlo Giannini. Upon completing his electrical engineering degree, he decided on impulse to try drama school as a way of overcoming his shyness. Acting became his profession and in 1975 he turned up in American theaters as a star in the movie *Swept Away*. . . .[5]

You may not become an international movie star by practicing with your scripts, but you can take inspiration from the many actors and actresses who've overcome their shyness and entered a demanding industry with great success. Use their devices to battle shyness in *your* life.

7

The Fine Art
of Friendship

I hope you've been working diligently on your shyness exercises. Because one of the best rewards for your efforts in overcoming your shyness is expanding the extent, strength, and support of your social network.

SHYNESS AND FRIENDSHIP

The old, shy you probably doesn't have very many friends.[1] As Amy, a participant in one of my studies, sadly noted about her lack of friendships, "Since the tenth grade I've taken the attitude that I can't be bothered making friends. All the anxiety I had to go through seemed a waste."

Perhaps most of your emotional support has come from your family. And what about the friends you do have? Studies tell us that most shy people feel their friendships don't provide the understanding, affection, support, empathy, and attention that shy people crave.[2] To make matters worse, your shyness keeps you from taking advantage of social opportunities—places and times when new friendships can be developed.

The barriers to making friends are all built from the components of shyness I've talked about in previous chapters. To quickly recap:

• Low self-esteem: Unless you begin to feel good about yourself, you won't realize that others are interested in knowing and calling you a friend. Shy behavior protects your self-esteem. A low profile enables you to avoid disappointment and embarrassment, but at a high cost: loneliness and isolation.

• Fear of rejection: You cannot reach out to others when you're worried about whether or not you'll be accepted.

• Self-absorption: Obsessive attention to your own thoughts and behavior prevents you from getting accurate feedback from others. It keeps you focused on your own unrealistically high expectations concerning your own behavior.

These barriers also affect how others perceive you, decreasing your chances for friendship. Several studies have examined how shyness is interpreted by the non-shy. In one study, interviewers described shy participants as "worrying, weak, frail, and reticent." They also underestimated shy people's intelligence. Roommates of shy students also gave negative descriptions: "self-pitying," "defensive," "overly cautious," "self-defeating." About the only people who described the shy in a positive light were their spouses, who've had the time to get to know the person behind the shyness.[3]

All this misperception creates a vicious circle. Your shyness makes you uneasy in social situations. Others misinterpret that as aloofness, which adversely affects their evaluation of you. The only way for you to break out of the vicious circle is to work hard on the exercises in this book, to consciously choose to change your behavior, and to continue using those exercises as you step out into the social world.

SOCIAL REWARDS OF FRIENDSHIP

Friendships are vital to the enjoyment of life. They provide what psychologists call *social rewards*—attention, respect, praise, sympathy, and affection—the stuff that money can't buy.[4] Because we're such a social species, there are times when even the simple presence of another person is rewarding.

The price we pay for gaining social rewards is "payment in kind." Part of earning the respect of others is to treat them with respect; to have praise bestowed on us we must recognize others' accomplishments; to gain sympathy, we must show warmth. Perhaps as an extension of their own self-criticism, shy people are often judgmental toward other people—they have difficulty with the "you scratch my back, and I'll scratch yours" concept that sustains friendship.

Social rewards imply give-and-take; you can't passively receive them. It's not enough to smile and nod during conversation. Occasionally you must *respond,* to show that you're interested and alert. Sometimes you have to be the initiator. Otherwise, you're at the mercy of those around you, always waiting for *them* to make the first move.

WHAT'S YOUR BALANCE?

No one likes to feel isolated and lonely. But does that mean that every minute of each day must be filled with the presence of other people, with the giving and receiving of social rewards? Of course not. Each of us needs time alone and time with other people. How much leisure time should you devote to solitary hobbies? How much to friends? There's no right or wrong answer. Each person has different needs. Some want to spend more time with other people than alone; others require greater amounts of private time. Only you can determine what your optimal balance is.

You're out of balance when you watch TV or read a book or work on your stamp collection when you'd *rather* be in the company of friends. When loneliness, boredom, or restlessness set in, then it's time to adjust your balance.

Your ideal balance ebbs and flows over time. If you work in a busy office surrounded by people, your private time may be a priority. A job without much social interaction, on the other hand, may spur you to fill more of your leisure hours with friends. Some periods in your life require you to withdraw from an active social calendar, to take time for introspection. At other times the whirl of social activity keeps you feeling alive and growing.

In your self-development notebook, describe your current ideal balance. In the space of a week, how much private time do you need for yourself? How much social time? How much time are you spending alone when you'd rather be with other people? Make up your mind now to work at creating your ideal balance.

RISKS AND REWARDS OF FRIENDSHIP

Any human relationship can hurt us. A friend may hurt us with words or deeds, betray a confidence, or choose not to fulfill a request. We despair at the demise of a close friendship. Sometimes we grow apart from a friend, as each of us changes and goes off in new directions—these partings are no less painful than a friendship that comes to an abrupt end.

If there is so much potential for hurt, why are friends so highly valued? Because friends are essential to life. The rewards of friendship are worth the risks of hurt. A true friend offers the closeness of a lover, spouse, or family member without being totally enmeshed in our lives. Friends help us to see perspectives and viewpoints through their eyes. They enrich our lives and promote our growth. Friends share the ups and the downs of our lives, lend a shoulder to cry on, give a pat on the back for achievements, impart their own words of wisdom and advice, and add a sparkle of fun to our daily existence.

TYPES OF FRIENDS

We label all types of people as "friends." We may consider a co-worker a friend, even though we don't see him or her outside office hours. We might call our next-door neighbor a friend, though most of our interactions are comprised of making arrangements for feeding pets and watering plants while one of us vacations. A classmate might be a friend, even though after graduation we lose touch.

Friend is a label we apply indiscriminately—from those who are actually mere acquaintances and new people in our lives we hope to cultivate as friends to those few whom we bare our souls to. Different friends fulfill different needs in us. A coworker, better than anyone else, may completely understand the frustrations of work and the excitement of new projects or promotions. A long-standing friend shares our past history and can relive with us the "good old days." New friends know us as we are now; they get the best (and worst) of us without having seen the process of our growing maturity.

Many people count as friends, each one rounding out an aspect of our lives. To a certain extent the boundaries of friendship are set by the two individuals involved. For example, you may get to know someone whom you'd like to develop a close friendship with. But this person may not have the time to invest in a new, close friendship or may be unable to open up enough for the intimacy friendship requires. An easy, casual friendship therefore becomes the accepted format. Some friendships develop rapidly, with personal details of life shared almost immediately. Other people become friends slowly, as the public face we present drops slowly to mutually reveal the many different facets of our personalities. Every friend needn't be a "close friend"—but close friends are the ones that mean the most.

THE QUALITIES OF CLOSE FRIENDSHIP

Mutual trust and respect, support, affection, dependability—these are the prime qualities of close, intimate friendship. Yet they aren't the *foundation* of friendship. Joel Block, a psychologist who conducted an extensive study of friendship in the late 1970s, describes three ingredients of friendship.[5]

First is *authenticity*—the freedom to be yourself, without pretense, without worrying about what "face" you should present. It's the freedom to relax and simply be the real you.

Second is *acceptance*. Without the safety net of acceptance, it would be difficult to feel free enough to express the range of your feelings and thoughts. Friends accept not only the good things about us, but also our faults. If we had to worry about being judged or condemned, we'd hold back. An Arabian proverb expresses in a lovely way the concept of acceptance: "A friend is one to whom one may pour out all the contents of one's heart, chaff and grain together, knowing that the gentlest of hands will take and sift it, keep what is worth keeping and with a breath of kindness blow the rest away."

Third is *direct expression*—telling a friend what you need, what you'd like. A friend won't always be able or willing to fulfill every request, but it's better to be open about what you expect than to rely on manipulation or indirect communication. Direct expression is also the sharing of positive feelings, telling a friend just how much he or she means to you. And it's expressing more difficult emotions—hurt and anger. "I felt hurt when you didn't invite me over to meet your old high school chum." "I got mad when I found out you'd told Gary about my demotion—I don't want everybody to know about that." Expressing your feelings directly keeps the lines of communication open and doesn't force your friend into playing mind-reader.

Authenticity, acceptance, and direct expression must be reciprocal between two friends. It may sound corny, but the Golden Rule seems to me to be the embracing principle of strong friendship: "Do unto others as you would have them do unto you."

THE SPOILERS OF FRIENDSHIP

Shy people need to be aware of two potential spoilers of friendship. The first involves a lack of appropriate *self-disclosure*.[6] I talked about this in Chapter 5, and I want to reemphasize here how important self-disclosure is to building friendship. If you encourage a new friend to confide in you, to tell you about his innermost thoughts and feelings but never share your own thoughts, ideas, and feelings, the relationship will be out of balance. Your friend will be left feeling vulnerable and exposed. You'll know a great deal about him, but he'll know little about what motivates you and what matters most to you. The power in the relationship will reside with you instead of being equitably distributed.

I know that learning to share your thoughts and feelings with other people may seem very difficult. When you're used to keeping your thoughts to yourself—thus avoiding any risk of rejection—it takes conscious effort to change your pattern of relating. It may take some time for you to feel safe sharing yourself with a friend.

The second potential spoiler of friendship is *overdependency*. Because shy people typically have a limited circle of friends, they may rely too heavily on one or two people to satisfy their friendship needs. Part of the dissatisfaction that shy people often feel with their current friendships is the direct result of demanding too much from too few friends.

When you count on one person to be everything—constant companion, confidant, helper, advice giver—he or she often burns out. You're asking too much from one person. You need to build up a network of friends and acquaintances, sharing your leisure time and pursuits with several people.

HOW FRIENDSHIPS ARE FORMED

Social psychologists have for many years studied how and why we get to know the people we do. Not surprisingly, it's the people we encounter with regularity who are most likely to become our friends. It's the fellow student who always sits next to you in class, or the coworker you see daily at the coffee machine, or the neighbors who live closest to you. As you see the same people each day or week, they become more and more familiar and less and less strangers. It becomes easier to strike up a conversation, to gradually get to know them. (Of course, if for some reason you took an initial dislike to someone, repeated encounters are unlikely to change your first feelings.) It seems that our friendships occur almost randomly, with whoever is repeatedly in our environment.

Your emotional state also affects how you respond to new people. When you're feeling happy and upbeat, you're more likely to appear approachable, and to react with positive emotion to strangers. And when you're feeling cranky or depressed, you won't be in the mood for getting to know a new person. Even though a stranger in your presence isn't responsible for either your good or bad mood, your feelings of the moment will color your perception of him or her and whether you'll make the effort to be friendly.

Another major factor in forming friendships is your need to make new friends. If you have a great many friends you probably won't expend the effort to get to know the person you bump into every day at the bus stop. But if initially you both feel neutral or positive toward one another, and both of you desire to extend your circle of friends, then your daily encounters may lead to the beginnings of a friendship.

Suppose you see the same person regularly, suppose you're generally in a positive mood, and suppose you're interested in making new friends—what determines if your initial acquaintance with this stranger will develop into a friendship? In early encounters with a potential friend, conversations consist mostly of comparing attitudes. Do you both share a similar outlook on life? Enjoy the same pastimes? The same music or literature? In general, the more similar the two of you are, the more you'll like one another and the greater the likelihood that you'll become friends.[7] This doesn't mean that two friends must agree on everything (that would be boring!), but the greater the proportion of beliefs and values that two people share, the more they tend to like one another.

This outcome usually extends to personality similarity as well. While we're often told that opposites attract, research shows that those who have similar personality characteristics have happier and longer-lasting relationships. This makes sense: A submissive person soon tires of being constantly directed by a dominating friend. A cautious person is soon worn out by attempts to restrain an impulsive friend. The closest of friendships are usually with people similar to oneself.

Friendship's final determinant is how much another person likes you and expresses positive feelings about you. We all like to hear words of appreciation and warmth (except when it's obviously false flattery). When a person evaluates you positively, you like them! Even dissimilarities in your attitudes or personalities can be overlooked when liking and respect for one another are communicated at the same time.

GETTING OUT AND MAKING FRIENDS

Now that you know a little bit about friendships and how they're formed, it's time for you to make a plan for expanding your social network. Going out with the vague notion of making friends probably won't get you far. And it's too easy to say to yourself, "I'll work on that later," and never get around to it. You've got to examine your resources, determine your needs, decide on concrete action, and put yourself in the right frame of mind.

Two important resources to consider are your time and financial position. Long work hours and/or home obligations mean that you need to figure out how best to budget your time. After your work time, "maintenance" time (grocery shopping, household chores and repairs, etc.), and private time, how many hours in a week do you have left over for leisure activities? Use the chart that follows to determine your number of leisure hours in a week.

	MON	TUE	WED	THU	FRI	SAT	SUN
Work	—	—	—	—	—	—	—
Maintenance	—	—	—	—	—	—	—
Private Time	—	—	—	—	—	—	—
Sleep/Rest	—	—	—	—	—	—	—
Total hours	—	—	—	—	—	—	—
Hours left over for leisure	—	—	—	—	—	—	—

Your chart should now show you how many free hours you have each day to do as you'd like. You'll also need to consider your energy level and how that matches up with your available leisure time. When are your best hours? Perhaps you have enough hours left over at the end of a work day to take an evening class. But if your energy level is typically low after a day at work, a weekend class might serve you better.

Now that you've got an overall picture of your "playtime" hours, let's break it down even further. The next question to ask yourself is how many hours of your leisure time do you want to commit to meeting new people and cultivating new friends? Ideally, you want to work out a balance between pursuing your solitary hobbies (reading, sewing, gardening), spending time with established friends, and extending yourself in new directions to meet new people.

My total leisure hours per week: ____

I want to spend
____ hours pursuing solitary hobbies/activities
____ hours with my established friends
____ hours getting out and meeting new friends

Start with your estimated time for friendship building, but allow yourself the freedom to decrease or increase the amount of time as you go along. You might find that you've allotted too many hours to friendship building and that you're pushing yourself too fast. Or you might find that you're really enjoying stretching yourself and increase your amount of time. However many hours you decide to devote to friendship networking, keep a log in your self-development notebook of your hour goals, what you did, and your level of enjoyment.

Another consideration is your financial resources. Unfortunately, getting out and doing usually costs money, whether it's the price of a movie ticket or tuition for a class. As you begin making your plans, consider how much of your income you can reasonably allot to this venture. But don't let money stop you—there are many ways to get out and network without spending your life savings.

WHERE TO MEET PEOPLE

You meet compatible people by doing the things you like to do. If you consider that we most like being with people who are similar to us, then the wisdom of this advice becomes clear. You're also more likely to relax, have fun, and feel most like yourself when you're involved in an activity that you genuinely enjoy.

So, what do you like to do? Here's a list to get you started thinking about what you enjoy.[8] Check off any of the activities or interests that you currently enjoy or think you might like to try your hand at. (This list is far from complete, so by all means add your own activities.)

☐ acting	☐ foreign languages
☐ animals/pets	☐ fashion
☐ art appreciation	☐ music appreciation
☐ astronomy	☐ piano, guitar, etc.
☐ auto repair	☐ photography
☐ gardening	☐ communications
☐ hiking	☐ crafts
☐ camping	☐ sewing/knitting
☐ dance	☐ gourmet cooking
☐ radio	☐ flying
☐ downhill skiing	☐ boating/sailing
☐ cross-country skiing	☐ genealogy
☐ swimming	☐ horseback riding
☐ tennis/racquetball	☐ karate/judo
☐ bicycling	☐ opera

☐ motorcycles   ☐ singing
☐ nature study   ☐ theater
☐ bridge/cards   ☐ drawing/painting
☐ carpentry   ☐ home repairs
☐ designing   ☐ walking
☐ interior decorating ☐ jogging
☐ writing   ☐ antiques
☐ editing   ☐ stamp/coin collecting
☐ calligraphy   ☐ basketball/volleyball
☐ pottery/ceramics   ☐ embroidery
☐ chess   ☐ softball
☐ _____   ☐ _____
☐ _____   ☐ _____
☐ _____   ☐ _____
☐ _____   ☐ _____
☐ _____   ☐ _____

Of the activities and interests you checked off, and your own additions, which ones actively involve other people? Those are the ones you'll want to consider participating in—they're the activities that will lead to potential friendships.

Adult education classes are one of the best sources for finding a class or seminar on an activity that you already enjoy or want to try. Usually these classes have a modest tuition fee and are offered by local colleges and county governments. Classes give you the advantage of repeated exposure to the same group of people for an extended period of time, and at each class meeting you can choose to sit next to the person whom you'd like to get to know. (Remember, proximity leads easily to introductions and casual conversations.)

Other places to find interesting groups and organizations to join are the Yellow Pages; newspapers; and grocery store, drugstore, and library bulletin boards. Also look for local or regional chapters of your profession's trade association. These organizations provide wonderful opportunities not only to keep up-to-date with your profession, but also afford an easy entrance into meeting and talking with your peers. Another often overlooked meeting ground is volunteer work. You can give your time and skills to those who need it, as well as making contact with other people who share your skills and interest in helping.

What Kind of Friends Are You Looking For?

Before you set off on your quest for new friends, think about what kind of friends you're lacking.[9] Do you want more same-sex friends, or is there an absence of opposite-sex friends in your life? Are you seeking close friendships or more casual friendships—people to hang out with and share activities with? Are you looking for a friend to share the same passion for a specific hobby?

As you consider your needs, keep your eyes open for any new people who look like they'll be the type of friends you're seeking. I know this sounds cold, practical, and efficient. But remember that you're trying to balance your social life. If you already have a few casual friendships, is another casual friend really going to make you feel more satisfied when what you want is a closer friendship?

Pull out your self-development notebook and set your goals. You've figured out your number of leisure hours and how many of those you'd like to devote toward friendship-building. You've been thinking about what activities you really enjoy and which ones involve other people. You've now got some ideas about where to look for your preferred activities, and exactly what types of friends you need in your life. Write it all down—and go after it. And remember to give yourself rewards for each step in the process.

_____

Keep a Positive Mental Attitude

Just before you set out for your adventure, take a few minutes for a PMA (Positive Mental Attitude) session. Whatever your day's been like—good, bad, or indifferent—sit down, relax, and focus your thoughts on anticipating positively your free-time activity.

If you like, review the social-skills tips in Chapter 5 to refresh your memory. Decide that the best result of the event would be meeting someone new who might become a friend. The worst outcome is that you'll have participated in something you enjoy and perhaps even learned something new. Either way, you can give yourself a pat on the back for getting out of the house and making an effort.

You're on Your Own

You're probably not going to like this piece of advice, but it's essential that you *go alone* to whatever activity you choose. Tempting as it is to persuade a friend to join you, you'll only defeat your purpose. If you've got a friend with you, chances are you'll end up talking only to your friend instead of making the effort to meet new people.

If you join a club or organization that divides up into smaller groups to plan activities, volunteer to be on a committee. For example, suppose you join a skiing club and a group is formed to plan the midwinter ski weekend. By being a part of that group you'll have a specific task to focus on and you'll be interacting with a smaller group of people. It's very likely that you'll get to know your fellow committee members quite well as you work together.

If just reading this is making your knees knock together, here's an exercise you can practice to warm up. Whenever you're in a situation where there are strangers, practice making conversation. Even this might seem scary, but remember, you'll probably never see them again. It doesn't matter what a stranger thinks about you. This is just for practice.

For instance, I once traveled alone to Washington, D.C., for a long weekend break over the summer. On the flight from Boston to Washington, I sat next to a gentleman from New Zealand. At first I thought he wouldn't be the talkative type, but not long after we were airborne he asked me if I was familiar with Washington National Airport. We spent the rest of the flight chatting about his work and mine. He was a very interesting person who'd traveled extensively, and the flight passed quickly and most pleasantly.

On my return trip, I arrived at the airport almost an hour early for my flight, and in the waiting area fell into conversation with a woman from Scotland. She regaled me with stories about her children and how she came to marry an American and make her home in the United States.

On the flight itself, by chance I was seated next to a young woman who had graduated the year before from the college where I work. It was another opportunity to engage in light conversation and spend the time pleasantly.

Three lively, interesting people: I'll probably never see any of them again, but each made my traveling time enjoyable and fun.

You'd be surprised how friendly most people really are. Take small opportunities for making brief conversation with passing strangers and I think you'll find a lot of your anxiety and fear disappearing with each new encounter. Talk to the person behind you in line at the grocery or department store; say hello to the person waiting at the bus stop with you; smile and make a comment about the restaurant to the person also eating alone at the next table. Dare yourself to take a chance. You'll soon become expert at meeting and chatting with new people.

EXTENDING INVITATIONS

After you've chatted with someone on several occasions and decided that you'd like to get to know the person better, what do you do next? Is the fear of rejection stalking forward from the back of your mind? You can't guarantee acceptance or even continuing friendship with every invitation, but there *are* some things you can do to minimize the risk of being turned down.

As you chat with new acquaintances, use open-ended questions to draw them out. Find out what other activities or interests they have. Are there other areas you share in common? Do they already have a close friend or group of people they share these activities with? Does it seem as though that group is expandable or already at its limit? Does a new acquaintance talk about a bevy of friends?

The answers to these questions will inform you of how much in common you share with another person, whether joining in on his or her other activities is open or closed, and whether or not it sounds as though they've already got a full social calendar. If you've encountered a busy, socially active person who has more friends than he or she can keep up with, extending an invitation may lead to a "no, thank you." Better to target your energies elsewhere.

When you find someone who is open to making new friends, shares many of your interests and views, and has time to spend with you, it's time to take a chance. Use the script-writing technique from Chapter 6 to work out the wording of your invitation and practice it until you feel fairly comfortable and relaxed. Your invitation can be general or very specific, depending on the situation and the approach you want to take.

Let's say you've taken a five-session class learning to play racquetball. Over the five weeks you've talked to one person in particular at each class, and you'd like to invite him to play racquetball with you soon. The general, but straightforward, approach would be something like this: "Nick, I've enjoyed getting to know you a little bit during our classes. I'm wondering, would you be interested in getting together sometime soon for a game?" Nick might answer, "Yes! That'd be great. Let's set a time right now." Or, Nick's response might be equally general: "Sure, we'll keep in practice together." With a general answer, you'll either have to interpret it as an elusive "no" or press for a specific time and see what kind of response you then get.

If you're getting good vibes from your new acquaintance, you may feel comfortable enough to extend a specific invitation. After a course in growing your own vegetable garden, you decide you'd like to make a specific invitation to a fellow gardener. You say, "Rachel, I've enjoyed meeting you! I'm planning a trip to a new nursery this Saturday afternoon. Would you like to come with me?" Rachel's response could be very positive: "Oh, the new nursery on route 35? Yes, I'd like to go with you. What are you planning for your garden?" Or: "Oh, I already have plans for Saturday. By any chance would you be willing to go on Sunday? I'm free then." Of course, you may also get a polite "no, thanks" in one form or another.

If you get a "no" or a vague answer that means "no," don't despair. Remind yourself that there are any number of reasons for someone declining your invitation. At the end of a class or seminar, the person may decide that the activity wasn't of interest to them after all. They may not want to pursue it any further; they tried it and didn't like it. Perhaps they're shy too, and don't know how to communicate that they *are* interested in becoming your friend. Or, you could simply be mismatched.

When you get a "no, thanks," check with yourself to see if you were aiming too high or too low—were you expecting too much, too soon, from your new acquaintance? Did you phrase your invitation negatively? "You probably won't be interested, but would you like to . . ." Were you falling into the trap of overemphasizing the risks (rejection) and undervaluing the rewards (acceptance of your invitation)?

Whatever the case, chalk it up to experience and *don't* put yourself down as unlikable. Give yourself a nice reward for trying, and keep on trying. Instead of slipping into self-criticism, think about baseball: When a baseball player is a .300 hitter, we feel he's great. But if you think about it, being a .300 hitter means that the player hits the ball only thirty percent of the time. And that's the way you've got to think about your efforts: If you get a thirty-percent acceptance rate, you're doing great. So, don't let the misses get you down, and continue working toward your hits.

FRIENDSHIP: A FINAL THOUGHT

In addition to all the joys friends bring into our lives, they also open up new avenues to us. Friends have friends, and your social network expands as you meet your friends' friends. Sometimes someone who's "just a friend" suddenly becomes a romantic interest. And, in fact, it's often our friends who introduce us to that one special person in our lives.

CHAPTER 8

Making Romantic Connections

As we enter the 1990s America is experiencing the so-called man shortage, AIDS, and the end of the sexual revolution. Numerous books on the never-ending battle between the sexes tell us that there are women who love too much, men who hate women, women with a "Cinderella Complex" and men with the "Peter Pan Syndrome." In the face of all these obstacles to connubial bliss, shyness seems like the last straw.

There's nothing worse than feeling tongue-tied and inadequate around the opposite sex. There's nothing so dreaded as the thought that you'll never make your romantic connection. As Pam, one of my study participants, said, "I don't think shyness is cute when a twenty-two-year-old woman is afraid to approach a man she likes." Whether you're single and not currently dating, recovering from a broken relationship, involved in an unhappy affair, or alone through divorce or widowhood, use this chapter to assess your romantic prospects and give yourself a real chance in the dating game.

MEN, WOMEN, AND SHYNESS

A few years ago I appeared on a New England radio talk show to discuss shyness. During the listener-response time, a young woman called in and asked me about this problem: "When my girlfriends and I go out to clubs in the evening, we find that a lot of the men stand off to one side. I'm wondering if the men want to ask us to dance, but they don't because they're shy. It's a very frustrating situation. What do you think of this?"

I told this caller that although both sexes suffer from shyness in roughly the same proportion, the consequences are different for men and women. The men in that bar may have been feeling shy. And even though women today feel freer to approach men, we still assume that the man will be the initiator, making the first move, showing the first signs of interest. This requires a fair degree of assertiveness and self-confidence—precisely what shy men lack. Consequently, for very shy men this lack results in fewer dates than it does for very shy women.

The radio-listener and her friends were waiting for the men to approach *them;* they weren't taking the initiative and asking the men for a dance. Male or female, shy or not, being the initiator means risking rejection. They chose not to risk rejection, but they missed an opportunity to meet available partners and to fully enjoy their evening out.

On the surface, it seems that shyness isn't the burden for women that it is for men in the dating game.[1] At first, a man might be intrigued by a shy woman, believing her to be the epitome of femininity. But a shy woman can also be viewed by a man as cold or aloof. He doesn't get the signs of interest he's looking for. He may give up or decide that the attraction isn't mutual. Therefore, the shy woman can just as easily fail to make her romantic connection as the shy man.

Very shy men may envy the woman's role.[2] She doesn't have to initiate, she doesn't have to risk rejection, she takes no chances. Women appear to have it easier. But there's a cost. She must wait to be chosen, and she may not feel free to take a chance and make a choice for herself.

Both women and men suffer under traditional roles. No one likes to be rejected, and no one wants to wait on the sidelines of life, waiting to be chosen. Fear of rejection is a real issue for both sexes.

It's not just a few extremely shy people who find it difficult to approach the opposite sex. In a 1978 study, University of Arizona psychologist Hal Arkowitz and his colleagues found that in a group of almost 4,000 students, thirty-seven percent of the men and twenty-five percent of the women said that they were "somewhat" or "very" anxious about dating.[3] Even normally confident people often feel a little shaky when they ask someone out on a date.

But shyness goes beyond feeling somewhat or very anxious about dating. Shy people date less frequently than their socially self-confident counterparts. They avoid situations where they can meet available people of the opposite sex, thus severely reducing their pool of potential mates.

In contrast to socially self-confident people who tend to play the field, shy people remain firmly attached to their dating partner.[4] Almost by default, they tumble into exclusive relationships before knowing if their partner is actually someone who suits them. Rather than facing the challenge of seeking a new, and perhaps more compatible partner, shy people will maintain an exclusive relationship to the bitter end. When an unhappy relationship winds to its finale, the results can be devastating as the barrier of shyness looms large again.

Shyness can also place an otherwise happy relationship in jeopardy. For example, a middle-aged woman named Leslie told me of moving away from the small town where she and her husband grew up so that he could take a better job in a large city. Her husband soon made new friends at work, while she, still job-hunting in a strange town, missed her old friends and acquaintances.

Cut off from her previous support and envious of her husband's social success, she was concerned—and quite rightly—that her marriage would suffer if she didn't find a way around her shyness.

Why do shy people fail so miserably in the scramble for dating and mating? It's due to the same stumbling blocks that I've talked about in earlier chapters. Shy people underestimate their level of social skills with the opposite sex. They allow their inner critic to take over, filling their minds with pessimistic, negative self-statements about their chances with a prospective date. Expecting to be flops, shy people anticipate that members of the opposite sex won't find them appealing. Shy people are merciless when it comes to evaluating and criticizing themselves for their behavior around other available singles.

All the exercises in Chapters 2 through 5 are designed to help you fight those stumbling blocks. In addition to those exercises, there are specific actions you can take to help yourself win in the dating game.

FINDING YOUR SOULMATE

Wouldn't you like to find someone whom you can talk with end-lessly about everything—and nothing? Someone you can snuggle up with at night? A confidant, best friend, and lover all in one? Someone who, above all, you feel free to be completely yourself with, and they with you? Sounds perfect, doesn't it?

Read the first sentence in the above paragraph again. The key word is *find*. Your soulmate isn't going to knock on your door one evening or weekend and say, "Hi, I'm here, sorry I'm late!" *Finding* your mate requires a practical approach. You'll need to make a plan, actively look, risk rejection, and date numbers of people until you find the right person.[5]

A "plan"? Isn't that just a little cold and calculating? Isn't love supposed to be something that knocks us off our feet all of a sudden? Isn't it destiny or fate? Aren't we supposed to suffer just a little bit in our search for love? Not necessarily. All our notions about romantic love (and unrequited love) are fed by TV, movies, books, and popular music. Finding love in the real world takes a lot of real effort and real work.

Let's begin by figuring out what, and who, you're really looking for.

WHAT KIND OF RELATIONSHIP ARE YOU LOOKING FOR?

Many people overlook this simple question and find themselves entangled in a relationship that isn't meeting their needs. They end up hurt, and so does the person they're involved with. You need to be brutally honest with yourself on this one, because the kind of relationship you're seeking will determine how you relate to the people you're attracted to.

It's often painful to be a single person in a double-occupancy world. Our culture says that two is better than one. "You're so nice and attractive, too—why aren't you married?" It's an intrusive question, and there's never any simple answer to it. It's tempting to swallow the bait and say that you do want to get married, you just haven't met the right person yet. I think it's better to go after what *you* want, not what other people think you should want.

What kind of relationship do you want? Do you want to casually date a few people? Become involved in a long-term relationship? Find a marriage partner? Someone to live with? Do you want no relationship at all? When you're thinking about the kind of relationship you want, avoid comparing yourself with friends, family, and coworkers. Discard the notion that there's a "best" age to have a steady boy- or girlfriend or a spouse. What other people choose for themselves is right for them. You have to choose what's best and right for you.

You may be able to answer the relationship question quickly. Perhaps you already know that you're the marrying kind or that you're not. Or it may take weeks or months for you to sort out exactly what kind of relationship fits your needs. Whatever answer you arrive at, it's important that you be honest with your dating partners.

This doesn't mean you should say on the first date, "If you're not interested in marriage then I don't want to see you again," or jump the gun by asking, "Where do you think this relationship is going?" or state emphatically, "By the way, I'm not into commitment." Usually the question of what direction a relationship is headed comes up naturally as the relationship progresses. If time passes and it doesn't come up, then it's entirely appropriate to bring up the subject. You don't want to spend a whole year with someone hoping for marriage only to find out that he or she has no intention of marrying you now or anytime in the near future. Nor do you want to mislead your partner about your intentions. There's no point in settling for a relationship that isn't what you truly want.

Begin a "Romance Section" in your self-development notebook and when you've decided what kind of relationship you're looking for, write it down.

WHAT IS YOUR IDEA OF THE PERFECT MATE?

Most of us carry around a vision of our perfect mate. We judge potential dates by this vision, sometimes almost unconsciously. On sight alone we may rule someone out. Or after one date we decide "No, he's not the one." We tell ourselves that the chemistry isn't there. Subconsciously we've compared a date with our vision and decided that important qualities are lacking. Sometimes it's difficult to say exactly who we *are* looking for or what makes the chemistry right.

Put your vision into words. In your notebook, make a list of the qualities your ideal mate has. Do this as quickly as you can, writing without stopping to consider whether one quality is more important than another, or even if it's appropriate for your list. Here's an example drawn up by my friend Riane.

MY PERFECT MATE

27–35 years old
very attractive
intelligent
minimum of a college degree
5'9"–6'3" tall
weight proportionate to height
physically fit
graceful/coordinated
broad shoulders
has my sense of humor or appreciates my humor
hardworking, with some ambition
average to moderate salary earnings
white-collar worker
sense of the outrageous
ability to share feelings
has own hobbies and interests
shares some hobbies or interests with me
honest
trustworthy
interesting nose

empathic
compassionate
engaging, happy smile
expressive face
fair (nonjudgmental)
relaxed, easygoing
ability to balance work, leisure, and family time (won't sacrifice relationship
    for career advancement)
enjoys sex
dark hair, blue eyes
likes self (but not egotistical)
loyal (wouldn't embarrass or criticize me in public)
accepts my friends even if he doesn't particularly like them
doesn't criticize my family unless I do
supportive of me and my ambitions

It's unlikely that Riane will find someone who has *all* the qualities and characteristics on her list. This, after all, is a description of a fantasy person, someone who doesn't exist. The point of writing out your specifications for an ideal mate is to get you consciously thinking about the person you're looking for.

A word of caution: The hallmark of shyness is unrealistically high expectations coupled with low self-evaluation. Research with shy men shows that they have a long and rich history of daydreaming about their fantasy woman.[6] She's physically perfect, sexual, loving, and caring. She has the body of Marilyn Monroe and the motherly kindness of Betty Crocker. The gap between fantasy and reality can make the daydreaming world an easier one to live in.

Similarly, many woman live their fantasy lives through literature. Witness the immense popularity of the romance novel. The hero is always handsome, sexy, and just a little bit dangerous. He exists in novels, but he can't be found in bars, at work, or in the apartment next door.[7]

Take this exercise seriously, but be realistic. Yes, it's easier to live in a fantasy world with your perfect woman or man. However, that won't get you any closer to a satisfying real relationship.

Here's your reality check: After you've compiled your list, think about all those qualities your ideal mate has and number them in the order of their importance to you. Which matters to you more —that your ideal mate is very attractive or intelligent? Is it more important that he or she has a sense of humor or supports you in your ambitions? In other words, since Mr. or Ms. Perfect is an impossible dream, what does Mr. or Ms. Close-Enough look like?

Would you rule out a potential mate because his or her age range was a year or two above or below your ideal? If you met someone who was honest, but not always sympathetic toward others, would that person be crossed off your list? If you've always thought you'd marry a businessman but met a blue-collar worker who otherwise fit your ideal, would you reject him? Would a woman who wants to marry and have children but continue her career be deemed unsuitable when your vision is a stay-at-home wife and mother?

Only you can decide which qualities are the most important. By looking at the combination of qualities that are high on your list you can see how choosy you're being. There's absolutely nothing wrong with being particular or having high expectations—you just have to realize that the more restrictions you have for your acceptable mate, the longer it will probably take you to find that person.

If you're adamant about finding someone who has almost all of the qualities on your list, perhaps you're using perfection as an excuse for having no relationship. You may need to reevaluate what kind of relationship you want. Rejecting person after person may be a roundabout way of saying to yourself, "Actually, no one will do right now. I'm not ready to become involved in any kind of relationship."

YOUR RELATIONSHIP EXPECTATIONS

In addition to expectations about an ideal mate, we also have expectations about the relationship itself. Sometimes it's our unvoiced relationship expectations that cause a romance to turn sour just when we thought we'd found the right person.

Whatever type of relationship you've decided is right for you, spend some time thinking about *how* you'd like that relationship to work. I don't mean that your expectations should be set in stone—certainly flexibility and compromise are crucial to the survival of any relationship. But you're better prepared to hammer out the day-to-day workings of your relationships if you're very clear about what you desire.

If you're looking for casual dating partners, how often do you envision seeing each person? How much contact is too much contact? If you're seeking a committed relationship, whether it's living separately, together, or married, how do you envision your lives actually working together? Do you expect your lover to call you every night? Be home when you get home? Would it be important for you to have time to yourself or with friends away from your lover? Or would you do just about everything together?

As you imagine yourself in a relationship, ask yourself what you need from a relationship and what is most important to you. Make a list of your wants and expectations. When you become involved with someone, you'll be able to negotiate your relationship needs clearly. For example, "I treasure the time we spend together. I also need time on my own—to visit my friends or take a drive through the country."

As you ponder your expectations, ask yourself, "Is this type of relationship the best one for meeting my needs?" A case in point involves a close friend of mine named Cindy, who at age thirty felt lonely and incomplete without a husband. She married quickly, but unfortunately several years later began divorce proceedings. After several months of living by herself, she wrote to me: "It's funny, but I feel much less lonely now than I did when I was married." Her marriage was supposed to stave off lonely feelings, fill a void in her life, but it wasn't enough. If some of your relationship expectations seem too high or unrealistic for one person to provide, perhaps you're asking too much from that person.

How can you tell if your expectations are too demanding? Sketch out a description of your ideal relationship in your notebook. Then look back at it and pick out the needs that this relationship would be fulfilling. Now think about your friendships, your relationships with family members—are some of these same needs being met in these other relationships? Or are you asking for all your needs to be met in one relationship by one person? Are you daydreaming or being realistic?

When you've given serious thought to the type of person you'd like to meet, the type of relationship you want, and the quality of that relationship, you're ready to begin your search.

LOOKING FOR YOUR ROMANTIC CONNECTION

There's no one best way to find a compatible partner, no magical formula to follow. People meet in just about every imaginable situation. For example, one of my friends met her husband on a ferry ride; another met his wife at a bar; another has known her husband since they were in high school together; another met his longtime girlfriend at work; and one of my brothers met his wife on a blind date. The fact is, there are any number of ways to meet available people.

Here are just a few ways of getting out and meeting other singles. Don't limit yourself to these methods alone; consider whatever seems most promising for your personal situation and then use your creativity and imagination!

• *Friends:* If you let your friends know you're looking, they'll probably be only too happy to introduce you to their single friends. Admittedly, some people seem to be more naturally skilled at matchmaking than others. A friend may set you up on a blind date, and to your amazement she's perfect. Or you may end up sitting in a restaurant wondering why your friend ever thought you'd be interested in the man sitting across the table from you. Let your friends know you're looking, tell them what type of relationship you're seeking, and ask them if they know anyone they could introduce you to. Friends are a good resource for networking with other single people and they provide a more personal introduction to potential mates.

If you're saying to yourself, "But I don't have friends like that," go back to Chapter 7. Friendships should be the foundation of your social life, not a resource you only rely on when you're in between dating partners.

• *Work:* As more and more women enter and remain in the work force, the workplace is increasingly becoming a meeting ground for singles. There are hazards, however. It can become awkward being involved with a coworker. Others in the office may resent the relationship, especially if one of you holds a higher position in the company. If the romance fails, you have to consider what it'll be like seeing your former lover every day at work. If wedding bells toll, many companies don't allow spouses to work together.

Still, don't rule out work as a possibility for meeting someone. Just be aware of the pitfalls and approach any liaison with caution. You can show some discretion by not advertising to the whole company who you're dating (though your close coworkers may guess anyway). And many companies are beginning to take a more lenient attitude toward couples who meet and marry while under their employment.

• *Outside activities:* Remember all the ways I told you about for meeting new friends in the last chapter? Those are the same activities that may lead you to finding someone special. A clear advantage to meeting people in this way is that there isn't a lot of pressure. You're there because you're interested in the activity; your focus isn't on meeting *The One.*

For example, a friend of mine named Marilyn met her future husband one Sunday afternoon on a nature walk at a local park. Marilyn's goal was to enjoy an autumn day, but it led to much more.

• *Personal ads:* Although the popularity of personal columns has increased, many people are still reluctant to try them, considering it risky and a waste of time. If you place an ad yourself, you reduce any risk by responding only to the letters that you feel comfortable with (most personal columns provide a post office box for respondents to reply to and then forward the letters to you). When answering an ad, you don't need to give your address or last name—just your first name and telephone number. If you're worried about weirdos, choose an upscale magazine to place your ad in or respond to one. The cost of a personal ad can be about sixty dollars for a ten-word ad. That's an expensive way for people with less than honorable intentions to get their thrills.

When placing an ad or responding to one, be honest about yourself. If you have children, you should say so. If you're more than a little overweight, you should mention it. Losing your hair? Admit that you're balding. Anything that would make a difference to you when meeting someone for a date is something that's worth mentioning when you advertise or reply to an ad. Both you and your date will avoid disappointment with honest self-appraisal.

• *Dating services:* A reputable dating service provides a specified number of introductions for a price. Be aware that dating services can be costly. Some agencies use videotapes so you can see another client's self-introduction and then decide whether or not you'd be interested in a date with that particular person. Others don't use videotapes or photographs, instead matching people up solely on the basis of personality similarities and interests. If you're interested in trying a dating service, look for one that has been in business for at least a few years. Ask your other single friends if they've ever tried a dating service, and if so, which one and what their experience was like.

• *Singles organizations:* Many large cities have organizations that provide a meeting ground for singles. Some are oriented toward a specific activity, like biking or dancing. Others organize a variety of outings for their members to join in. Perhaps the one disadvantage to a singles organization is that despite the activity at hand, the focus *is* on meeting a dating partner. But don't rule out singles organizations. Go to a few different singles events and see if their ambience feels comfortable to you.

• *Classes on relationships:* Your local Y, community college, or adult education school most likely offers a variety of courses dealing with relationships. Some of them are very specific—for example, a workshop on dating—and some are targeted to relationships in general. Through these classes you'll meet other people who experience many of the same difficulties you do, share solutions, and get practical advice from the workshop or seminar leader. Best of all, you'll realize that there are many other singles who are willing to meet together and discuss ways out of the loneliness trap.

Try two or three of the suggestions above at the same time. Remember: *Go alone!* It's much more difficult for you to meet potential dates if you've got your best friend in tow. The more people you come in contact with, the more dates you go out on, the faster you'll find someone compatible. Dating will sometimes be fun, sometimes a bore, and sometimes anxiety-provoking. You've got to take the bad dates with the good, and remind yourself that you're actively looking—and that's hard work.

YOUR ATTITUDE TO DATING

Your mental approach to dating could mean the difference between success and a single bed. Common wisdom has it that when you're *not* looking for a mate, things suddenly start to happen. That's because you're more relaxed. Whenever you go out with the resolution "Tonight, I *am* going to meet someone, the right someone," then failure and disappointment are sure to follow. A desperate state of mind isn't going to attract anyone.

So, how do you look for a dating partner without appearing to be looking? When you go out, tell yourself "I'm ready to meet the right person." But don't tell yourself that it will happen at this party or that club meeting or seminar. Give yourself every chance to meet potential dates, and be open to the possibility of meeting Mr. or Ms. Right—but not desperate.

If you shouldn't appear desperate for a relationship, should you play hard-to-get? Elaine Walster and her colleagues wanted to find out why the hard-to-get woman is so appealing to men.[8] She found that it's the *selectively* hard-to-get woman who wins the dates. While a hard-to-get woman represents a challenge to men (and prestige if a date is secured), she may also appear to be too "cold" and "choosy." The easy-to-get woman is a guaranteed date, but men often fear that such a woman will become too dependent, too demanding, too serious. A selectively hard-to-get woman combines the best of both. She is not easily available to all men, but she's choosy enough to go out only with the men who genuinely interest her. Men, it seems, are attracted to women who are hard for other men to get.

Although this study only looked at dating from the male perspective, I wouldn't be surprised if the results would be the same for women and the hard-to-get man. Female or male, each of us likes to feel that we're chosen above all others.

APPROACHING THE OPPOSITE SEX

It happens. You see someone who's definitely a possibility. What do you do now? All of a sudden all those exercises you've been working on to overcome your shyness seem to have left you. You feel hopelessly inept, your stomach turns somersaults, you can't think of a thing to say.

Here are two tips for getting yourself beyond the first rush of attraction. First, stop looking at the opposite sex as alien beings. When you see a man or a woman who attracts you, look at him or her as a person. *Look beyond gender, and approach the person as an individual.* What is this person thinking, feeling? What kind of personality does he or she have? The sum total of any of us extends far beyond our gender.

Second, whether it's love at first sight or a sudden change of heart about someone who had been "just a friend," recognize that what you're experiencing is physical attraction. There's nothing wrong with that. But think to yourself, "Okay, I'm physically attracted to this person. Let's see if there will also be a mental attraction that could develop into an emotional attachment." Instead of becoming flustered by intense attraction, you can approach the person calmly with the idea that it would be wonderful to explore the possibilities of a meaningful relationship.

Fine. You've steadied yourself. Now, what do you say?

OPENING LINES

I mentioned Chris Kleinke's work on shared conversational time in Chapter 5. He's also studied what kinds of opening lines women and men prefer.[9] Kleinke had over five hundred people write down all of the opening lines they could think of for both general and specific situations. Next, he had more than one thousand volunteers rate each opening line from "terrible" to "excellent."

Three categories of opening lines emerged: cute-flippant, direct, and innocuous. Kleinke found that neither women nor men like cute-flippant openings. But he also discovered that men don't realize how much women dislike cute-flippant openers. A cute-flippant opener is an aggressive way to approach someone. And women, he also found, believed that men like innocuous openings more than they actually do. Here are some of his examples of each kind of opening line:

CUTE-FLIPPANT

"You're probably wondering what a nice guy like me is doing in a place like this."
"I bet the cherry jubilee isn't as sweet as you."

DIRECT

"Since we're both sitting alone, would you care to join me?"
"I feel a little embarrassed about this, but I'd like to meet you."

INNOCUOUS

"What do you think of the band?"
"The weather is beautiful today, isn't it?"

Kleinke's advice to men: Use innocuous lines if you're not in the mood for a possible rejection, and use direct openers when you're feeling confident. For women he advises greater use of direct lines. It seems that when a woman uses an innocuous opener, men aren't sure whether or not she's expressing an interest in them or in just making conversation.

You don't have to approach someone you're attracted to with a witty, sexy, or funny opening line. Something quite ordinary will be perfectly fine. I told a friend of mine about Kleinke's study, hoping to encourage him in his romantic endeavors, but he remained apprehensive. "What if I use one of the opening lines you suggest to a woman at a bar and she says, 'You jerk, get lost!'?" All I can say to that is: Why would you want to know someone like that anyway? Lucky you found out what a jerk *she* is before you got past the opening line. You can't allow one rude person to stop your search for a mate.

ASKING SOMEONE OUT

There's a right and a wrong way to ask someone out on a date. Don't just walk up and ask, "Are you busy Friday night?" That's an awkward and intrusive request for a date, and practically begs for rejection. Instead, select an activity you think your potential date might enjoy, then approach the person, stating the outing you have in mind, when you want to meet, and why he or she might enjoy it, closing with the question, "Would you like to go?" This approach doesn't force your potential date to admit he or she has no plans for a Friday night—and in the event that the person's busy, it leaves the door open for another encounter. "I'm sorry, I already have plans for Friday, but I'd love to go folk dancing with you next weekend."

This is a perfect point at which to use the script-writing method from Chapter 6. Whether you're planning a face-to-face or telephone invitation, write out your request-for-a-date script, practice it out loud to yourself, and thereby increase your confidence when the time comes to do the actual asking.

An additional dating tip: Make it a short date. Instead of planning a lengthy outing, arrange a limited daytime activity, lunch date, or drinks after work. The other person is more likely to say "yes" to a cup of coffee than to a long evening out. A short date gives both of you a chance to get to know one another under a more relaxed setting than the traditional Friday or Saturday night date.

By whatever means you arrange a first date, make every effort to suspend judgment of your date after your first meeting alone. Too often singles make snap decisions about each other; no one wants to waste a minute of time if a date doesn't appear to be perfect. It's almost impossible, however, to know on the first date whether or not someone is a strong candidate for a relationship. Unless your date really turns you off, I'd suggest at least a second rendezvous when both of you will be a little more relaxed.

WHAT DO YOU TALK ABOUT ON A FIRST DATE?

It's your first date with someone special. What do you talk about? What if both of you sit there in uncomfortable silence? What if the whole afternoon or evening is a disaster—all because you couldn't keep up your end of the conversation?

First, review the social-skills tips discussed in Chapter 5. Remember to self-disclose so your date can get to know you better, and don't let worries about what you'll say when it's your turn to speak get the better of you. Use the empathic listening and responding techniques. And keep reminding yourself that you're talking to a person, not just a member of the "mysterious" opposite sex.

New research by Mark Leary, a psychologist at Wake Forest University, provides a key to the first date and conversational techniques.[10] Leary gave a group of shy people instructions for their first conversational encounter with a stranger: Find out as much as you can about the other person. Not only did his shy participants feel better about the interaction, but so did their conversational partners.

Put yourself in your date's shoes and think of a few possible topics of conversation before you meet. What does she like to do in her spare time? What does he think is the best aspect about his job? What social issues concern her most? What would you like a date to know about you? Approach your conversation as an exploration. Talk about the things that you'd talk about with your friends.

Dates somehow seem more trying than other social situations. Every social encounter has the possibility of rejection, but rejection from a member of the opposite sex is even more painful. Being turned down for a second date has subtle undertones of being judged an inadequate woman or man, a less-than-desirable mate. When a date doesn't work out, chalk it up to experience and *keep on dating!* You'll probably have to date many people before you find someone compatible, so don't let a disappointment set you back.

SHYNESS AND SEX

It seems that everyday social inhibitions extend to the bedroom for some shy people. In my research I've found that shy people tend to suffer from higher levels of sexual anxiety and guilt than the non-shy.[11] Sexual pleasure often seems out of reach for them. Sex involves a level of intimacy that exposes more than our bodies— our strongest feelings and passions are exposed, making us utterly vulnerable to another human being.

Even though shy people score just as well as the socially self-confident on objective tests of knowledge about sex, shy people *think* they're less knowledgeable. Because sex has a strong performance component to it, Mark Leary and his colleague Sharon Dobbins attribute shy people's low self-ratings to self-doubts about their expertise in bed.[12] Yet like the unrealistically low ratings shy people give themselves for social skills, shy people may also underestimate their sexual skills.

Making sex more enjoyable can take some of the anxiety away for the sexually shy. Therefore, first things first: If you don't know how to protect yourself from pregnancy, venereal disease, and AIDS, make an appointment with your physician or local Planned Parenthood clinic. When you're confident about your birth control method, and have assured yourself that you've taken all necessary precautions against disease, you'll feel a lot more comfortable with your partner.

If you're one for lights out during lovemaking but your partner likes to see you, recall from Chapter 3 that shy people rate themselves as less physically attractive than other people. You're probably underrating your physical attractiveness. Remember that very few people look like they just stepped out of the centerfold of *Playboy* or *Playgirl*. If you feel uncomfortable with your body and you skipped the mirror exercise in Chapter 3, now's the time to go back and do it. You've spent years feeling insecure about your body, so be persistent with the mirror exercise. A one-time shot at it isn't going to get you over a lifetime of insecurity. Let the mirror become your friend, become comfortable with looking at yourself, and in time you won't feel so embarrassed about your body in front of a woman or man.

Next, take a new romance slowly. Don't go to bed with a new lover until you feel very comfortable and confident that she or he can be trusted. Talk about sexual issues—pregnancy, venereal disease, and AIDS. Decide together how you'll protect each other before you turn back the covers. It's *not* unromantic to discuss these issues before you make love with someone. Talking openly about sexual health issues conveys your love and concern for another person.

Finally, work on becoming friends first, lovers second. Studies on marital longevity tell us that the married couples who are the happiest are those who count each other as their best friend.

THE LAST WORD ON FINDING LOVE

It seems as though overcoming shyness and finding love require a lot of effort. Yet the barriers produced by shyness are real. Research reveals that shy women and men tend to marry later in life or not at all.[13] If you do nothing to change the status quo, you allow the odds to remain stacked against you. However, the time and energy you devote to overcoming your shyness can result in a much better payoff.

Wouldn't you rather make your best effort than look back on your life with regrets? "If only I'd smiled at him . . . said something to her . . . gone to that party . . . signed up with a dating service . . . kept that rendezvous with the blind date . . ."

In the end, there is no guarantee that we'll find the love of our life. Give it your best shot, though, and enjoy the new people you meet along the way—even if none of them turns out to be the one for you. And always keep thinking positively about yourself and the next person. You never know, he or she could be *The One*.

CHAPTER 9

The Rewards
of a Career

Incredible as it seems, Lee Iacocca, the pugnacious chairman of Chrysler, was once a shy young man.[1] Needing to become more self-confident, he enrolled in Dale Carnegie seminars and changed his life. He describes overcoming his shyness as a crucial step in his career.

What would have happened to Iacocca if he hadn't vanquished his shyness? Maybe he would have become an auto executive. But could he have redeemed Chrysler's fortunes at the moment of the auto giant's greatest crisis? Could he have convinced management not to give up hope or persuaded union workers to restrain their contract demands if he couldn't deal with people confidently? I doubt it.

Not everyone, of course, can become another Lee Iacocca. And while Dale Carnegie classes worked for him, that doesn't mean they're the answer for every shy person. Nevertheless, his example demonstrates that with diligence and hard work, shyness can be overcome. You don't have to let shyness stunt your career growth.

HOW SHYNESS HURTS CAREERS

Underemployment—being stuck in a low-paying job that requires less skill or training than you possess—uneasy work relationships, and slower advancement mark the careers of shy people.[2] About two years ago, after I gave a lecture at one of the high-tech companies that dot the Boston area, Desmond, a thirty-two-year-old engineer, told me how shyness ruined his chances for getting ahead in his company. "I was up for a promotion and I didn't get it. My boss told me I wasn't outgoing enough for the position and that my communication skills were lacking." At the same event, Melissa, a recent college graduate, confessed to me that she worried about ever getting on a career track: "After graduation from college, I found it difficult to find a job because I was afraid—afraid of calling employers, afraid of interviews. My shyness held me back from going for a good job. Now I'm employed in a position for which I'm overqualified." Studies show that shy college students don't make use of campus career centers, recruiting opportunities, and academic advisors.[3]

Even highly trained professionals suffer in their workday life. Linette, a physician in a radiology residency program, says, "My self-consciousness and lack of social skills is absolutely debilitating. The other residents I work with must think I'm a real idiot."

Shyness hurts careers from the very beginning. Too shy to approach people who can guide them through the job-hunting process, shy people don't take advantage of available resources.

Doubting their worth, shy people typically apply for jobs below their skill level.[4] After all, they reason, how can you be turned down for a job you could do with your eyes closed? Also, because job interviews strike terror in them, they usually take the first job offered—whether or not they really want it. Accept that first offer, they think, rather than face another round of telephone calls, applications, interviews—and possible rejection.

Regardless of how little they enjoy their first jobs, shy people switch employers with great reluctance—yet switching companies is a tactic many successful people use to climb the corporate career ladder. Once employed, shy people often act passively, unwilling to take initiative or use their abilities to stand out from other employees. Networking (making contact with influential people in your career area) is recognized as *the* way to land a good job, as well as to advance your career. For most shy people, however, networking is an impossible dream.

Finally, shy people self-select themselves out of high-paying careers. Almost every lucrative career requires solid communication skills, an assertive personality, and an astute sense of office politics. Shy people invariably choose careers that don't require a lot of communication, ending up in jobs that reward them with neither status nor money.

Psychologists maintain that good psychological health is made up of love, friendship, and work. As we saw in the chapters on friendship and romance, shyness can stymie the growth of both companionship and love. In the career area, too, shyness creates enduring problems. Psychologist Robert Hansson of the University of Tulsa found that when shy older workers got laid off from their jobs, it took them longer to begin looking for a new job.[5] Hansson also found in his study that the more shy the worker, the less prestigious his last job title tended to be.

Do you avoid making career decisions? Do you avoid seeking advice and help from others in your career area? Do you dread the whole job-hunting game? Have you fallen into a job rather than planning a career? If these questions strike a nerve, pay attention— I'm going to suggest a whole new way of taking charge of your professional life.

WHERE DOES A CAREER FIT INTO YOUR LIFE?

There's an important difference in my mind between a job and a career. A job isn't a career—it's just something that brings in the paycheck. A career, on the other hand, has a goal—a level you desire to reach in your chosen field. Actively involved with your career, you keep up with new developments in your field, growing personally as well as professionally. A job may become your life work if you repeatedly postpone making a change. Before you know it, you end up doing the same job for all of your working years. There's nothing wrong with that, as long as you like your job and get some satisfaction out of what you do.

Do you have a job or a career? Which do you want? Is your work a means to an end—a means that provides money for the necessities of life and for pursuing your outside hobbies and interests? Or is it one of the major sources of satisfaction and meaning in your life? Only you can decide what you want. Whether you opt for a job or a career, your work should provide structure and stability, a source of identity (I'm a nurse; I'm a statistician; I'm a construction worker), and a social arena to share in with your coworkers.

Use your self-development notebook to write out some of your thoughts on job versus career, taking plenty of time to do this. Think it out carefully, talk about it with your friends. See where you come out on this important decision.

If you've decided that your work is a means to an end, then find a job that's reasonably satisfying and pays you enough to attain your ends, whatever they may be. For some people this really is the way to go. I remember when I worked on a construction project, saving my money for graduate school. One of my coworkers was a bright young man named Hank. One day while we were drinking coffee and munching donuts, I asked him why he wasn't working in the field he'd trained for in college. Hank explained, "Actually, I did have a job that related directly to my college degree, but it didn't pay well and it left me no time for activities outside work. Now I work here, building houses, for damn good money. I use my time outside work to follow my college interests as hobbies instead of making them my career."

But if, unlike Hank, you want a career that *matches* your interests, then you need a plan that will work for you. The first and most important step is figuring out what you want to do.

BUTCHER, BAKER, CANDLESTICK-MAKER

A lucky few seem to know what they want to do from an early age. For them, a career path is clear and their chosen vocations are also their avocations. They love what they do and they're usually happy with their work. Most of us, however, struggle to find work that gives us a sense of competency as well as challenge.

The greatest stumbling block to zeroing in on a career is, I think, the notion that you have to decide what *it* is, once and for all. Unless you're considering a career that requires graduate school—a large expense and time commitment—relax a little. Chances are that you'll probably change careers at least once in your working life, or move around within your career area. The best you can do is to figure out what you'd like to do now, and keep in mind that it's not a lifetime commitment.

You can always change careers five, ten, or fifteen years from now. Look at the many people who start new careers once they've retired from their lifelong work. In addition, with mergers and acquisitions, new technology, and two-career couples, you may find yourself changing jobs involuntarily or to accommodate your spouse.

Now let's get started. Here are the ways I want you to start thinking about designing a career.

• *Describe your dream job:* This is a fun way to help you focus on your interests and skills. You'll be surprised what you learn about yourself. You probably won't be able to find work that includes every item on your list, but you'll get a better idea of what you're looking for, and by prioritizing your list, you'll know clearly what's most important to you. In your self-development notebook, write out everything you can think of about your dream job. Don't worry about a specific title for your job, or whether or not you have the educational level to land the job. Let your pen fly over the paper as you list your requirements for your ideal job. For example, here's what my friend Gwen wrote down for her dream job:

Educational or nonprofit sector
40–50 hours per week
Health and retirement benefits
Some occasional travel would be fun
Mostly work alone, but also work with others
Managerial position
$30,000–40,000 annual salary
Reasonable vacation time
20% of job involves writing
Opportunity for advancement
Challenging—opportunities to learn more
Allows creativity within job
Variety in job tasks
Some interaction/work with other departments
Problem-solving tasks
Good work and effort recognized and appreciated
Work ultimately (directly or indirectly) helps others

• *Speak to other people:* Even if *you* can't determine what you should do with your career life, people close to you often can give you valuable feedback. Ask your friends, family, and coworkers,

"What do you think I'd be good at? What kind of career do you see me excelling in?" Sometimes other people, especially coworkers, are better at pinpointing your talents than you are. You may take for granted or not recognize some of your unique skills. Your friends could even suggest a career you never thought of. Even if none of your friends' ideas appeal to you, you'll undoubtedly end up finding out more about yourself.

• *Try vocational counseling:* If you're still stumped after the last two steps, consider vocational counseling. Even if you're starting to get a good idea of what you want but remain uncertain or undecided, try seeing a vocational counselor. The work you've done yourself—thinking about the tasks in your ideal job and talking with your friends or coworkers—hasn't been wasted; it will help you get more out of counseling.

Vocational counselors, whether in private practice or employed in university counseling programs, use paper and pencil personality assessments to match your skills and interests with people who are employed in various career areas. A good vocational counselor will also discuss with you where you think your interests lie, and exceptional ones will help you get started networking with a contact or two. Private vocational counseling costs money, but it can save years of frustration and anguish by enabling you to target your career and move ahead to establish yourself.

• *Utilize career centers:* Nearly every college and university has a campus career center. Although many centers advise only students, there's no reason why you can't ask for permission to use their libraries. These centers often have vocational literature that your public library may not carry. If you're still in school or taking a night course through your local college, take advantage of this resource. If you are a graduate of a college or university, avail yourself of their career centers.

• *Read vocational books:* When you don't have money for career counseling, or a good career center isn't available to you, head off to your local library and bookstores. There are many books available that will help you write résumés, brush up on your interviewing techniques, and assist you in figuring out what you want to do.

One of the best known and highly regarded is Richard Bolles's *What Color Is Your Parachute?* For a more comprehensive study on how career fits into your life, look at Bolles's *The Three Boxes of Life and How to Get Out of Them.* John Holland's book *Making Vocational Choices: A Theory of Careers* includes a self-scoring test to help you determine your career area. There are also guides with workbook formats such as Barry and Linda Gale's *Discover What You're Best At.*[6]

Be realistic about your career goals. You don't want to undervalue yourself, nor do you want to aim for a career that may be out of reach for you. If you're severely shy, public relations may not be a realistic career goal for you. On the other hand, if your life happiness depends on entering a high-communication field, then you know you're going to have to work extra hard on overcoming your shyness.

PLANNING YOUR CAREER PATH

Use your self-development notebook to write down your career plans in detail. If you don't already know what career you want to pursue, begin by setting out what steps you'll take to figure that out, using the suggestions I've just described. When you know what career path you want to follow, write down what you need to do to get there. Do you need more schooling, professional training? If so, where are you going to get it? You may need to begin researching colleges and universities offering programs that fulfill your further educational needs. What level do you want to reach in your career? Who can you talk to to find out more about your chosen work?

_____

NETWORKING: Your next step should be a plan for networking. Get in touch with as many people as you can who are working in your preferred area and begin informational interviewing. When you interview someone for information, it's just that. You're not asking for a job. Use informational interviewing time to find out everything you can about the career area you're interested in from people who are currently employed in that field.

A woman I know named Jamie graduated from college a few years ago and has been working as a secretary. Now she's thinking about going back to school and earning a master's degree in public administration. Realizing that she knew little about what public administrators actually do, and not knowing anyone who was a public administrator, Jamie asked her parents, friends, and coworkers for contacts. She came up with two names that way. Then she checked with her local university's school of public administration. She got the names of three graduates potentially willing to talk to her about their careers.

Jamie made appointments with three of the five people on her networking list. She called them, identified herself, explained how she got their name, and asked if they would be willing to spend half an hour with her talking about their careers. All of them agreed. Before each of the meetings, Jamie made out a list of questions, which she frequently scanned during her interviews. Some of her questions were: What exactly do you do as a public administrator? What aspect of your job do you enjoy the most? The least? Do you feel that your graduate program adequately prepared you for the work world? If you had it to do over again, would you do anything differently to prepare yourself for this career?

These three people happily shared their experiences and opinions with her. Jamie came away with valuable information and an improved sense of self-confidence. (Note: Jamie might have found out from her informational interviewing that the job requirements of a public administrator were *not* to her taste; this equally valuable information prevents heartache and wasted time and money pursuing the wrong career.)

Jamie also took advantage of the professional association of her career interest. She joined the area chapter to help expand her networking potential. She met people working in public administration, learned more about the profession, and kept up to date with the latest changes and advances in the field. Two of her best job referrals came at chapter meetings. All of Jamie's initiatives helped her get a better understanding of her field. Put into practice, the same resourcefulness will also be a tremendous help to you.

INTERNSHIPS: Obtaining an internship in a field that's hard to break into is a great way to get your foot in the door. Even for minimum or no pay, internships help you gain experience and learn more about the day-to-day workings of a particular career. You may find you love every minute of it—or you may decide you'd rather lie on a bed of hot coals than pursue that career further.

Make out a step-by-step plan for pursuing your career. Set your goals. For example, "I'll visit two universities each month to learn more about their programs." "I'll make contact with one new networking person each week or month." "I'll speak to one new person at each meeting of my professional organization." "I'll spend every other Saturday at the library investigating companies where I can intern or apply for jobs." And then *do it!*

MAKE THE MOST OF YOUR PRESENT SITUATION

If you're in a job for which you're overqualified, harness your dissatisfaction into meaningful activities. You can make the most of your present job by practicing new skills and behaviors. Use the social-skills tips and exercises described in Chapter 5 to get to know your fellow employees better. Take a genuine interest in them, and they're bound to find you interesting too. You may soon find your present job a friendlier place to be.

If your company posts new job opportunities, apply for those you're qualified for and interested in. Talk to the person who's conducting the interviews, or to his or her subordinates. Tell that person you're thinking about applying for the job, and find out what kind of person they're looking for and what the job entails. Don't pin all your hopes on getting the job, but use the opportunity to practice networking and interviewing. Terrifying as interviews can be, the more you interview the better you'll get at it (more about interviews in a moment). Armed with the inside information you got from your networking, approach the interview with confidence. It's just practice anyway. It doesn't matter whether or not you get the job—your goal was just to improve your interviewing techniques.

But practicing to get a better job is not all you can do in your present situation. Look around your office and ask yourself what you can do to take initiative. Where could you make improvements and innovations within the job you do now? Use your current job to become more experienced and confident about suggesting new ideas to your boss. It's the people who use their creativity, imagination, and initiative who get out of dead-end jobs. When your boss sees you taking the bull by the horns and making improvements she begins to think, "Hey, this person has a lot to contribute to our company! Where can we better utilize his skills so he'll really be able to use that creativity and ingenuity?"

THE JOB INTERVIEW

Shy people universally dread job interviews. Low self-esteem causes them to interview poorly. It's awfully hard to convince someone you'd be a great employee when you don't believe it yourself. Shy people get caught in the vicious circle of low self-esteem, devaluing their skills and settling for too little in the way of a job. When shy people compare themselves to their coworkers, they often believe others do better than they do.

The trap of low self-esteem is so powerful that it causes shy people to resist training in assertive interviewing techniques. They believe that assertiveness results in disapproval from a prospective employer. On the contrary, research indicates that expressing oneself assertively in a job interview results in a positive evaluation by the interviewer.

Personnel executives struggle to imagine shy candidates as happy, successful employees, since their low self-esteem and inability to project themselves as enthusiastic and capable people creates the impression that they're less competent, less suited for a job, and in need of more training than self-confident job applicants. In addition, interviewers assume, often correctly, that shy employees have difficulty establishing harmonious relationships with coworkers. That's why you must work on all aspects of your shyness to make your work life more fulfilling.

Interviewing *is* nerve-racking. I remember my admissions interview at my first choice in colleges, an elite East Coast school. I completely flubbed my opportunity. I didn't think about what the interviewer might be looking for—a capable and enthusiastic student who would make the most of their college. I spent my time worrying out loud whether the college would overlook my low SAT math scores and expressing concern about the college's language requirement. I didn't get accepted. I hadn't gone into the interview in a positive frame of mind. I resolved to plan ahead for my next interview by taking a positive attitude. I was ultimately successful in gaining admission to an excellent college on the West Coast.

Interviews don't have to be your nemesis. Much of the anxiety a shy person feels about job interviews comes from the idea that he is being evaluated. While that's true, you must realize that two can play this game. Why don't *you* evaluate your prospective employer? As he or she assesses your skills, personality, and capabilities for a job, you can ask yourself the following: "Is this a job position that I would enjoy and could make some contributions to?" "Does this employer seem like a good choice to work with?" "Will this job challenge and stimulate me?" Remember: A job interview should be a *mutual* evaluation.

Here's another trick to boost your self-confidence. Put yourself in the interviewer's shoes. If you were screening applicants for the job, what qualities and skills would you be looking for? In your mind, you can interview the interviewer, and present yourself favorably. For example, you might ask the interviewer, "What special skills does this job require?" The interviewer replies, "We're looking for someone who can juggle the demands of a busy office and establish priorities among various projects." You reply that you know just what she means and back it up with your own experience: "When I worked for the ABC Company, we would have some projects that had to be rushed through and others that we were given plenty of lead time on. My task was to delegate the projects to my staff and ensure that the rush jobs got through in time and that the ones with a longer lead time weren't lost in the shuffle of rush projects."

Your attitude going into a job interview is crucial. Psychologist Richard Heimberg and his colleagues at the State University of New York in Albany conducted a survey of vocational counselors and found that a large number of their clients habitually generated negative self-statements when thinking about an upcoming job interview.[7] For example:

- I feel less qualified when I think about the other applicants.
- I sound like I don't know what I'm talking about.
- I forgot the questions I was going to ask.
- I'm freezing up under the pressure.
- I won't be able to answer an important question.

Remember the exercises in Chapter 4 on self-statements? Here's another area where you can apply the same principles again. Instead of becoming pessimistic and negative about a job interview, use positive self-statements to mentally gear yourself up for an interview, and at the same time work on building up your self-esteem. Some of the positive self-statements Heimberg came up with are:

- I expect the interviewer to like me.
- This place needs someone like me.
- When I leave I will feel that I have done my best.
- This job would give me a good chance to get ahead.
- This job sounds interesting and exciting.

The best place to prepare yourself for a job interview is at home before the interview. Get a trusted friend or family member to role-play the interview with you. Together think of all the difficult questions you're afraid you'll be asked and have your role-playing companion play the part of the interviewer asking the tough questions. Run through your practice interview a few times, preferably spacing out your practice sessions over a day or two. You'll enter the interview feeling better prepared and you'll have practiced how to answer the questions you're certain the interviewer will ask. During the actual interview, you'll draw on your role-playing experience to present yourself as the best candidate.

An additional way to help calm yourself before a round of interviews is to use the relaxation and visualization process described in

Chapter 2. If you're not an early-developing shy person and skipped that chapter, go back and learn a relaxation method and the visualization techniques. Apply the techniques to yourself: Visualize yourself answering an employer's questions calmly and confidently, and presenting yourself as an enthusiastic and competent employee.

A final word: Remember the ground rules of interviewing. Dress professionally; many job experts recommend dressing not only for the interview but as if you were applying for an even higher-level job—the one you'd like to be promoted to eventually! Make sure your personal appearance is neat and clean and, of course, have an accurate and updated copy of your résumé in hand.

Applying and interviewing for a job position is a game. No matter how much you may dislike that idea, that's the way it is. Don't rail against the system—learn to use it! Remember the idea behind scripts in Chapter 6? Take on the role of an assertive, competent job seeker. Employers want to find the best qualified and personable candidate for the least amount of money. It's a process of matching yourself with the right job, convincing an employer that you *are* the right person, and negotiating your salary.

MONEY MATTERS: NEGOTIATING
A SALARY AND SEEKING A RAISE

This area makes most people cringe—shy and non-shy alike. Prospective employers typically ask you what salary range you have in mind. If you suggest a salary too high, you price yourself out of a job offer. If you ask for too little, an employer may believe that you aren't quite savvy enough and disqualify you on that account. If the salary you suggest is at the bottom of the range they have in mind, that's just what you may get. Therefore, the salary you negotiate is important. If you undersell yourself by several thousand dollars in annual salary, it will take you *years* to reach that level through raises.

Richard Bolles in *What Color Is Your Parachute?* details the steps of figuring out what salary range you should ask for when you're interviewing. His method involves a fair amount of research, but it pays off. See his book for the steps of researching salary negotiation. As a person overcoming shyness, you need to keep in mind that your low self-esteem and negative approach may nudge you toward asking for less than you're worth. That's one reason why you should take the time to research what other people are getting paid in your geographical area for similar jobs.

Asking for a raise is never easy. Most medium- and large-sized companies, however, have an annual review when supervisors evaluate performance for the year and recommend raises. This is the perfect opportunity for you to bring up the subject of a raise. If you work for a company that doesn't have an annual review system, make an appointment with your supervisor to discuss the matter.

You can boost your chances for getting a larger raise by keeping a log of your work activities. As you begin and complete work projects, note them down in your log along with the benefits they provide to the company. A list of your accomplishments helps you see yourself as an effective person.

When your supervisor sets a time for your performance review, give him a summary sheet of your accomplishments *and* a list of goals for the next review period. The summary sheet reminds your supervisor of your contributions and reassures him that you have definite plans for continuing your efforts on behalf of the company. This procedure also makes it easier for your supervisor to back up a request to personnel for a raise above the cost of living. He can say, "Look, this employee has worked hard and contributed a lot to our department. She's even mapped out a plan for continuing her efforts. Employees like her don't come along very often—we want to be sure we won't lose her to a competitor."

Your log will also prove valuable when you apply for a higher position or change companies. You can see exactly what tasks you did routinely, as well as the special projects you initiated or worked on.

GOING FOR A PROMOTION

When you don't ask for raises, you're seen as an unambitious person. Similarly, if you don't seek promotions or even ask for expanded responsibilities within your present job position, you're regarded as someone who isn't committed to the company. Shy people tend to think that they get passed over for promotions because they made some mistake. If you've been passed over for a promotion, it's more likely that you never gave your boss the chance to get to know you and value your work. Your boss may even think you're a snob because you don't socialize with your fellow employees.

Shy people often protest that they're loyal, hardworking employees. Sadly, quiet loyalty is easily overlooked. There's truth to the old saying that it's the squeaky wheel that gets the oil. You're not going to be appreciated if you hide your talents; you'll only hurt yourself. Keeping a low profile can keep you at the bottom of the company.

As you work on overcoming your shyness, you may find yourself growing out of your job and ready to take on greater challenges. Going for a promotion is just the same as applying for another job. It's networking on a higher level, researching the qualifications for the job, getting an idea of the salary range, and interviewing for the position.

Here again your log provides you with rich material for presenting your accomplishments and talents. Draw on your log to present yourself favorably in an interview and to show the interviewer that you're ready to take on bigger challenges. Remember, motivate yourself with positive self-statements and practice a few esteem-building exercises to get yourself in shape for the interview.

PUBLIC SPEAKING

Public speaking is torture for most shy people. Whether it's giving a quick presentation to your work group or a lengthier talk to the company at large, there will be times when you'll have to stand up and be the center of attention. Is it worth learning to become a confident public speaker? Consider the frustrations of Ryan, a shy market researcher. "At a presentation to upper management, I was so uncomfortable it negated the fine work I'd done. I have good contributions to make, but I can't seem to get the hang of public speaking."

Michael Motley, a professor of communications at the University of California in Davis, has some useful pointers on public speaking.[8] First of all, he claims that about eighty-five percent of people feel some anxiety about speaking in public. So it's not just shy people who worry about this—even your confident coworker in the office next door probably frets and worries before a presentation. But Motley says there are differences between the way anxious and confident people approach public speaking.

Nearly everyone experiences some physical arousal before making a speech. Your heart rate increases, you might feel a little shaky, and generally keyed up. Confident people, however, interpret their physical arousal as a sign that they're geared up for their speech. They use their anxiety as a harness and not as a block to speech. And it probably makes for a livelier, more concentrated presentation. Anxious people, though, view their physical arousal as a sign of fear and then begin imagining what the sources of that fear are. "I'll stumble over my words." "The audience won't like me because I'll do terribly." "Someone might ask me a question after my speech and I won't know the answer." The fears compound, becoming irrational and catastrophic. With each fearful thought physical arousal increases until you've got a vicious circle going full steam ahead.

Would you believe that most audiences don't even notice a speaker's physical arousal? It's true. There's a surge of physical arousal, lasting for about thirty seconds, that occurs when you actually start speaking. Because you're aware of the surge, you focus on it and don't realize that it subsides.

You can alleviate physical arousal by using your preferred relaxation method for ten or fifteen minutes before you begin your presentation. You can also make public speaking less terrifying by changing your views about speaking. Motley suggests looking at speech as communication instead of as a performance. You're standing up there to share your knowledge or ideas to an audience that is there because they want to know what you know. A performance attitude means that you're aiming for praise for your delivery rather than for the content of your speech. We've all heard enough politicians to know that those with good delivery don't always impart much information during their speeches. Motley believes that a conversational style is best, using your usual gestures and facial expressions and engaging the audience through the content of your speech.

Draw again on the exercises in Chapters 2 and 4. Learn to relax yourself a little before your speech; practice relaxation and visualization, imagining yourself making your speech clearly and succinctly. Instead of barraging yourself with negative self-statements just before your talk, tell yourself a few positive things. "I'm geared up—I'm ready for this." "I put a lot of time and work into preparing this, and I know my audience will appreciate the information I have to share with them."

TIPS FOR PREPARING A SPEECH

Don't just sit down and write a speech the night before you have to do it. Approach your impending presentation with careful planning and rehearsal.

First consider your audience. Are they there to be persuaded? Instructed? Aided in a decision-making process? Are they there to gain new knowledge, and if so, how much do they already know about the subject? That is, what can you leave out of your speech, and what content is it vital to include?

The first items to write down are the salient facts about your audience and the purpose of your speech. This will tell you what they'll need to know, what they'll be looking for, and in what order you should present your information. Then write down a few key ideas of your presentation—the major topics you'll want to tell your audience about.

Make an outline of the major points and jot down a few words or short phrases under each that you'll want to cover. Don't write everything out. If you write out your whole speech you'll end up reading it, which is a guaranteed way of putting your audience to sleep. You just want to have reminders of your key ideas, glancing down every now and then as you talk about point one, point two, point three.

There's an old axiom in public speaking that you should tell your audience what you're going to tell them, tell it to them, and then summarize what you've just told them. That's basic English composition in verbal form. Give your audience an introduction—who you are, what you'll be speaking about, and what you hope they'll get from it. Then give the contents of your speech, following it with a brief summary.

Practice your speech several times at home until you feel comfortable with it. Keep a conversational tone. Memorize your ideas, not the actual words (one exception is to memorize the first line of your speech; it may help reduce your anxiety during the first surge of arousal). Time yourself so you can be sure you're staying within your time limit. It's much pleasanter to cut down the content of your speech during practice than it is to be cut off in public before you're finished. If you want to do more to develop your public-speaking skills, consider taking a Dale Carnegie course or joining Toastmasters International (both are listed in your telephone book).

LABOR PAINS

Finding your niche in the world of work is difficult. As a shy person you've got to work doubly hard at it. Study after study shows that shyness is a barrier to successful career development. But it's a barrier you can overcome if you choose to put in the time and effort necessary to make meaningful progress toward developing your potential.

Your career is an important source of self-esteem. Not everyone wants to be a million-dollar-a-year salesperson, so whatever career you choose, judge it against your *own* goals, defined by your values. Don't compare yourself to others. Compare yourself to what you know you can do, and then make the most of yourself and your career.

CHAPTER 10

Postscript: The Secret of Your Success

Although it takes time to overcome shyness, it *is* a battle you can win. Committing yourself to change means that you're opening up a whole new door for yourself: relating in new ways to people, feeling happier with yourself, moving more freely through the social world, enjoying the warmth and companionship of friends, the special bond with a lover, and the satisfaction of meaningful work in your life. In short, you're saying "No!" to standing on the sidelines of life.

STILL FEELING SHY?

There are two broad goals of self-development. The first is increasing your sense of self-acceptance: Yes, you're a shy person inside. The second is adapting your behavior to social situations: Forging ahead *despite* feeling shy. The shy part of you wants to avoid social encounters altogether—forget adapting! But your life-driving force wants to reach out and connect with other people. Now that you've reached the end of this book, perhaps you're saying "Yes! I want to make that human connection—*but I still feel shy.*"

Don't give up on yourself. Whenever you despair of ever being able to overcome your shyness, remind yourself that:

- You may always feel a little bit shy inside. Use your shy feelings as a signal to practice your relaxation technique, decentering, and new social skills.
- Your symptoms of shyness aren't nearly as visible to others as you may think.
- It's good to accept positive feedback! Rather than focusing on the negatives, seek your social rewards.
- Turning a disappointing social encounter into a learning experience will keep you on track. Notice what triggered your shyness, and continue to work on that situation step by step.
- Being your own worst critic will keep you stuck in the shyness rut. Be kind and fair to yourself.
- Striving for improvement in your behavior, rather than for perfection, will keep you engaged in a more fulfilling social life.

Remember to step back from time to time and look at the big picture. Your goal should *not* be a wish to wake up one morning transformed into the extroverted life-of-the-party. Set a realistic goal. Your time, energy, and effort should lead you toward being able to approach social interactions calmly and confidently. Make your match between your ideal self and your real self a possible, attainable goal.

Finally, if you haven't done the exercises in the previous chapters, then it's no wonder you may still feel shy. The exercises are a tool; they're a way for you to practice new behaviors and new ways of thinking about yourself. Use them!

Research stands behind the exercises. They *will* help you overcome your shyness. And employing a combination of different types of exercises is far superior to any one method by itself.[1] Without intentional, purposeful change on your part, as practiced through the exercises, shyness will continue to dominate your life.

(If you're interested in reading more about the process of making changes or other life issues I've touched upon, refer to the Suggested Reading section at the end of this book.)

STARING DOWN DEFEAT

You might think that overcoming your shyness is the most difficult thing in the world to do. In reality, it's breaking through your feelings of defeat and hopelessness that will prove to be your toughest challenge. You'll have to fight hard to prevent yourself from giving up before you've even tried to make any changes.[2]

You must realize that your shy behavior is reinforcing. When you avoid social encounters, you're probably thinking to yourself, "I can't handle this. I don't know what to do or say. It would be just awful if I made a fool of myself." Thinking of possible catastrophes actually provides an escape for you. You avoid the social situation, and so you feel relieved. You didn't make a fool of yourself—because you weren't there.

This brings us to the issue of short-term gains versus long-term losses. Your short-term gain is simple: By avoiding a social encounter, you saved yourself from any potential social embarrassment. The long-term loss is permanent, however. You've lost a chance to make contact with other people, an important element that's missing from your life.

It's a natural human tendency to opt for the short-term payoff, even if it's not the best choice for us in the long run. That's why you may find it hard to motivate yourself to do the exercises in this book. If you've been having this problem, work through the following levels of involving other people in your program.

First, recruit a friend or family member to help you. Ask them to role-play your difficult social encounters with you. Involve them in your goal plans, and report back to your helper on a regular basis with your progress and next goal plan.

If the first level isn't an option for you, or you need more structure, join a communication workshop or social-skills class. These are offered by community colleges, YMCAs and YWCAs, and community adult education centers. For a structured format that will push you harder, enroll in a Dale Carnegie course or join a Toast-masters club.

If you exhaust all of these levels and are still finding it impossible to make changes, consider seeking professional help. There are some extremely shy people for whom this level should be the first choice. Although the number of people who enter counseling is up dramatically from the 1950s, the vast majority of people who are debilitated by personal problems never seek help from a counselor.[3] This is a shame when there are thousands of qualified professionals available to help people out of their misery.

GETTING OUTSIDE HELP

It takes real guts to admit to yourself that you need outside help. Yet strangely, once you've made this admission to yourself and decided to find a counselor, there's an accompanying sense of relief. New research shows that reading self-help books often leads people to conclude that wishing to change a particular problem area of their lives is an important incentive for them to enter therapy. Therapists, too, see self-help books as a bridge between individuals sitting alone with their problems and getting help. In fact, a recent survey reveals that many therapists now recommend self-help books to their clients, believing that they can be helpful to their clients' growth and change.[4]

Finding the right person to work with does take some research. Ask your minister, doctor, teacher, or close friend for a recommendation. If those avenues aren't open to you, consult your telephone directory for local professional associations; they'll provide recommendations. You may also be able to find a referral from a new organization called the Anxiety Disorders Association of America (ADAA). Their address is PO Box 42514, Washington, DC 20015–0514. ADAA maintains a registry of human service professionals who specialize in treating anxious individuals. Therapy can be short- or long-term, on an individual basis or in a group. You'll want to discuss with your therapist your needs and goals, and work together in determining what will prove most beneficial for you.

Getting yourself into therapy is a Catch-22 situation for shy people. You may wonder how you'll be able to make and keep a first appointment with a therapist when you feel so shy. To make the phone call, use the script from Chapter 6. Then take your copy of this book with you to your first appointment and tell your therapist that this is what you've been trying to work on. Describe the different shyness symptoms and which ones are the biggest problems for you.

You may, in the end, decide that you *don't* want to put the effort into overcoming your shyness. That's certainly an option. At the minimum, you know a lot more about shyness now than you did before, and you can always come back to this book later when you feel ready to make some changes. But in the meantime remember this: *If you choose not to make the effort, don't be bitter about the consequences.*

THE FINAL ANALYSIS

Our culture is one in which shy people face two battle fronts. Our society worships the individual, encouraging self-absorption for those who buy into the notion of rugged individualism. (Not suprisingly, this self-absorption has been linked with the rise of depression in America.)[5] Even without the nod of social approval, shy people fall too easily into the trap of self-absorption. At the same time, they feel unable to compete with more aggressive social climbers.

A way to wage war against self-absorption is by engaging in a little altruistic behavior. A new wave of research on altruism shows that those who help others feel better about themselves, and that those good positive feelings are even reflected in better physical health.[6] Reach out to others in small ways—smiling, saying hello, showing interest in them. And reach out in larger ways—give your time and skills as a volunteer to a cause you believe in.

Your second battle is with yourself. Remember that overcoming shyness is a step-at-a-time process. Always keep in mind that the rewards for breaking out of your lonely world of shyness will be worth the effort you expend. Reward yourself for accomplishing each move forward, and when you turn around and look back, you'll see just how far you've come.

Reference Notes

Introduction
1. Philip G. Zimbardo, *Shyness.* Reading, MA: Addison-Wesley, 1977.
2. Jonathan M. Cheek and Arnold H. Buss, "Shyness and Sociability." *Journal of Personality and Social Psychology,* 41 (1981): 330–339.
3. Jonathan M. Cheek and Lisa A. Melchior, "Measuring the Three Components of Shyness." Paper presented at the 93rd Annual Convention of the American Psychological Association, Los Angeles, CA, August 1985.
4. Jonathan M. Cheek and Alan B. Zonderman, "Shyness as a Personality Temperament." Paper presented at the 91st Annual Convention of the American Psychological Association, Anaheim, CA, August 1983.
    "Shyness: How It Hurts Careers and Social Life" in *U.S. News and World Report,* October 31, 1983.
5. Warren H. Jones, Jonathan M. Cheek, and Stephen R. Briggs, eds, *Shyness: Perspectives on Research and Treatment.* New York: Plenum Press, 1986.

Chapter 1

1. Jonathan M. Cheek and Lisa A. Melchior, "Shyness, Self-Esteem, and Self-Consciousness." in H. Leitenberg, ed., *Handbook of Social and Evaluation Anxiety.* New York: Plenum Press, 1990.

    Jonathan M. Cheek and Arden Watson, "The Definition of Shyness: Psychological Imperialism or Construct Validity?" *Journal of Social Behavior and Personality,* 4 (1989): 85–95.

2. Jonathan M. Cheek, "The Revised Cheek and Buss Shyness Scale." Unpublished manuscript, 1983, Wellesley College, Wellesley, MA 02181.

3. For a review, see Jonathan M. Cheek, Andrea M. Carpentieri, Thomas G. Smith, Jill Rierdan, and Elissa Koff, "Adolescent Shyness." In W. H. Jones, J. M. Cheek, and S. R. Briggs, eds., *Shyness: Perspectives on Research and Treatment.* New York: Plenum Press, 1986.

4. Jonathan M. Cheek and Lisa A. Melchior, "Measuring the Three Components of Shyness." Paper presented at the 93rd Annual Convention of the American Psychological Association, Los Angeles, CA, August 1985.

5. Arnold H. Buss, "A Conception of Shyness." In J. A. Daly and J. C. McCroskey, eds., *Avoiding Communication.* Beverly Hills, CA: Sage Publications, 1984.

6. Arnold Buss, *Social Behavior and Personality.* Hillsdale NJ: Lawrence Erlbaum Associates, 1986.

7. James J. Lynch, *The Broken Heart: The Medical Consequences of Loneliness.* New York: Basic Books, 1977.

8. Jonathan M. Cheek and Catherine M. Busch, "The Influence of Shyness on Loneliness in a New Situation." *Personality and Social Psychology Bulletin,* 7 (1981): 572–577.

9. D. P. Morris, E. Soroker, and G. Burruss, "Follow-up Studies of Shy, Withdrawn Children—I. Evaluation of Later Adjustment." *American Journal of Orthopsychiatry,* 24 (1954): 743–754.

10. Peter R. Harris, "The Hidden Faces of Shyness: A Message from the Shy for Researchers and Practitioners." *Human Relations,* 37 (1984): 1079–1093.

11. Jerry A. Schmidt, *Help Yourself: A Guide to Self-Change.* Champaign, IL: Research Press, 1976.

Chapter 2

1. Stella Chess and Alexander Thomas, *Temperament in Clinical Practice.* New York: Guilford Press, 1986.
2. Jonathan M. Cheek and Alan B. Zonderman, "Shyness as a Personality Temperament." Paper presented at the 91st Annual Convention of the American Psychological Association, Anaheim, CA, August 1983.
3. Robert Plomin and Denise Daniels, "Genetics and Shyness." In W. H. Jones, J. M. Cheek, and S. R. Briggs, eds., *Shyness: Perspectives on Research and Treatment.* New York: Plenum Press, 1986.
4. Jerome Kagan, Steven Reznick, and Nancy Snidman, "Biological Bases of Childhood Shyness" *Science,* 240 (1988): 167–171.
   Allison Rosenberg and Jerome Kagan, "Irish Pigmentation and Behavioral Inhibition." *Developmental Psychobiology,* 20 (1987): 377–392.
5. Jonathan M. Cheek, Lisa A. Melchior, and Brian Cutler, "Eye Color and Shyness: An Application of the Three-Component Model." Unpublished manuscript, 1987, Wellesley College, Wellesley, MA 02181.
6. Jerome Kagan and J. Steven Reznick, "Shyness and Temperament." In W. H. Jones, J. M. Cheek, and S. R. Briggs, eds., *Shyness: Perspectives on Research and Treatment.* New York: Plenum Press, 1986.
7. William Angoff, "The Nature-Nurture Debate, Aptitudes, and Group Differences." *American Psychologist,* 43 (1988): 713–720.
8. John B. Watson, *Psychological Care of Infant and Child.* New York: W. W. Norton, 1928.
9. Kimberly L. McEwan and Gerald M. Devins, "Is Increased Arousal in Social Anxiety Noticed by Others?" *Journal of Abnormal Psychology,* 92 (1983): 417–421.
10. If you find that the systematic desensitization exercises don't help you stay calm in social situations, you can ask your doctor about the new developments in drug therapy for social anxiety. If your doctor is unfamiliar with this new research, you can refer him or her to the work on the MAO inhibitor phenelzine reported by Dr. Michael R. Liebowitz and his colleagues in the *Journal of Clinical Psychiatry,* vol. 49, 1988, pp. 252–257.
11. Gustav Friederich and Blaine Goss, "Systematic Desensitization." In J. A. Daly and J. C. McCroskey, eds., *Avoiding Communication.* Beverly

Hills, CA: Sage Publications, 1984.

G. M. Rosen, R. E. Glasgow, and M. Barrera, "A Controlled Study to Assess the Clinical Efficacy of Totally Self-Administered Systematic Desensitization." *Journal of Consulting and Clinical Psychology*, 44 (1976): 208–217.

Wes W. Wenrich, Harold H. Dawley, and Dale A. General, *Self-Directed Systematic Desensitization*. Kalamazoo, MI: Behaviordelia, 1976.

Joseph Wolpe, "The Systematic Desensitization Treatment of Neuroses." *Journal of Nervous and Mental Disease*, 132 (1963): 189–203.

12. Stephen M. Kosslyn, "Stalking the Mental Image." *Psychology Today*, 19 (May 1985): 22–28.

13. Encyclopaedia Britannica, "Methods of Relaxation," Instant Research Service.

14. Herbert Benson with Miriam Z. Klipper, *The Relaxation Response*. New York: Avon Books, 1975. Adapted by permission of William Morrow & Co., Inc.

Chapter 3

1. Jonathan Cheek, Andrea M. Carpentieri, Thomas G. Smith, Jill Rierdan, and Elissa Koff, "Adolescent Shyness." In W. H. Jones, J. M. Cheek, and S. R. Briggs, eds., *Shyness: Perspectives on Research and Treatment*. New York: Plenum Press, 1986.

2. Helen M. Johnson, *How Do I Love Me?*, 2nd ed. Salem, WI: Sheffield Publishing, 1986.

3. Nathaniel Branden, *How to Raise Your Self-Esteem*. New York: Bantam Books, 1987.

Diane Frey and C. Jesse Carlock, *Enhancing Self-Esteem*. Muncie, Indiana: Accelerated Development, 1984.

Matthew McKay and Patrick Fanning, *Self-Esteem*. New York: St. Martin's Press, 1987.

4. F. Ishu Ishiyama, "Origins of Shyness: A Preliminary Survey on Shyness-Inducing Critical Experiences in Childhood." *Journal of the British Columbia School Counsellor*, 7 (1985): 26–34.

5. Wendy E. Liebman and Jonathan M. Cheek, "Shyness and Body Image." In J. M. Cheek (Chair), *Progress in Research on Shyness*. Symposium

conducted at the meeting of the American Psychological Association, Anaheim, CA, August 1983.

6. Louise M. Mamrus, Cheryl O'Connor, and Jonathan M. Cheek, "Vocational Certainty as a Dimension of Self-Esteem in College Women." Paper presented at the 54th Annual Meeting of the Eastern Psychological Association, Philadelphia, PA, April 1983.

7. Jonathan M. Cheek, Lisa A. Melchior, and Andrea M. Carpentieri, "Shyness and Self-Concept." In L. M. Hartman & K. R. Blankstein, eds., *Perception of Self in Emotional Disorder and Psychotherapy.* New York: Plenum Press, 1986.

8. Stephen L. Franzoi, "Self-Concept Differences as a Function of Private Self-Consciousness and Social Anxiety." *Journal of Research in Personality,* 17 (1983): 275–287.

9. Barbara E. Breck, "Selective Recall of Self-Descriptive Traits by Socially Anxious and Nonanxious Females." *Social Behavior and Personality, II* (1983): 71–76.

10. Robert M. Arkin, Elizabeth A. Lake, and Ann H. Baumgardner, "Shyness and Self-Presentation." In W. J. Jones, J. M. Cheek, and S. R. Briggs, eds., *Shyness: Perspectives on Research and Treatment.* New York: Plenum Press, 1986.

   Mark R. Leary, *Understanding Social Anxiety.* Beverly Hills, CA: Sage Publications, 1983.

11. Daniel Goleman, "Research Affirms Power of Positive Thinking." *The New York Times,* February 3, 1987.

12. Carol R. Glass and Cheryl A. Shea, "Cognitive Therapy for Shyness and Social Anxiety." In W. H. Jones, J. M. Cheek, and S. R. Briggs, eds., *Shyness: Perspectives on Research and Treatment.* New York: Plenum Press, 1986.

Chapter 4

1. Reproduced by permission of MGM/United Artists Communication Company from *Annie Hall* by Woody Allen, copyright 1977.

2. Lisa A. Melchior and Jonathan M. Cheek, "Shyness and Anxious Self-Preoccupation During a Social Interaction." *Journal of Social Behavior and Personality,* 5 (1990): 127–140.

   Alice P. Arnold and Jonathan M. Cheek, "Shyness, Self-Preoccupation, and the Stroop Color and Word Test." *Personality and Individual Differences,* 7 (1986): 571–573.

Jonathan M. Cheek and Sherin Stahl, "Shyness and Verbal Creativity." *Journal of Research in Personality,* 20 (1986): 51–61.

3. Jonathan M. Cheek and Lisa A. Melchior, "Are Shy People Narcissistic?" Paper presented at the 93rd Annual Convention of the American Psychological Association, Los Angeles, CA, August 1985.

4. Charles G. Lord and Philip G. Zimbardo, "Actor-Observer Differences in the Perceived Stability of Shyness." *Social Cognition,* 3 (1985): 250–265.

5. Lynn Alden, "Attributional Responses of Anxious Individuals to Different Patterns of Social Feedback: Nothing Succeeds Like Improvement." *Journal of Personality and Social Psychology,* 52 (1987): 100–106.

6. Lorne M. Hartman, "Social Anxiety, Problem Drinking, and Self-Awareness." In L. M. Hartman and K. R. Blankstein, eds., *Perception of Self in Emotional Disorder and Psychotherapy.* New York: Plenum Press, 1986.

Georgette K. Maroldo, "Shyness and Alcohol Response Expectancy Hypothesis—Social Situations." *American Psychologist,* 41 (December 1986): 1386–1387.

7. Gordon H. Bower, "Mood and Memory." *Psychology Today,* 15 (June 1981): 60–69.

8. Jerry L. Deffenbacher et al., "Irrational Beliefs and Anxiety." *Cognitive Therapy and Research,* 10 (1986): 281–292.

9. Carol R. Glass and Cheryl A. Shea, "Cognitive Therapy for Shyness and Social Anxiety." In W. H. Jones, J. M. Cheek, and S. R. Briggs, eds., *Shyness: Perspectives on Research and Treatment.* New York: Plenum Press, 1986.

Marvin Goldfried, Edwin T. Decenteceo, and Leslie Weinberg, "Systematic Rational Restructuring as a Self-Control Technique." *Behavior Therapy,* 5 (1974): 247–254.

10. See, for example, Norman J. Kanter and Marvin R. Goldfried, "Relative Effectiveness of Rational Restructuring and Self-Control Desensitization in the Reduction of Interpersonal Anxiety." *Behavior Therapy,* 10 (1979): 472–490. Also Warren Ricks, Robert McLellan, and Catherine Ponzoha, "Rational-Emotive Therapy versus General Cognitive Behav-

ior Therapy in the Treatment of Low Self-Esteem and Related Emotional Disturbances." *Cognitive Therapy and Research,* 12 (1988): 21–38.

11. Carol R. Glass, Thomas V. Merluzzi, Joan L. Biever, and Kathy H. Larsen, "Cognitive Assessment of Social Anxiety: Development and Validation of a Self-Statement Questionnaire." *Cognitive Therapy and Research,* 6 (1982): 37–55.

   Marvin R. Goldfried, Wendy Padawer, and Clive Robbins, "Social Anxiety and the Semantic Structure of Heterosocial Interactions." *Journal of Abnormal Psychology,* 93 (1984): 87–97.

12. Lynn Alden and Robin Cappe, "Interpersonal Process Training for Shy Clients." In W. H. Jones, J. M. Cheek, and S. R. Briggs, eds., *Shyness: Perspectives on Research and Treatment.* New York: Plenum Press, 1986.

13. Thomas D. Borkovec, "What's the Use of Worrying?" *Psychology Today.* 19 (December 1985): 59–64. Reprinted by permission of *Psychology Today.*

14. Pamela Adelmann, "Possibly Yours." *Psychology Today,* 22 (April 1988): 8–10.

Chapter 5

 1. Jonathan M. Cheek, Lisa A. Melchior, and Andrea M. Carpentieri, "Shyness and Self-Concept." In L. M. Hartman and K. R. Blankstein, eds., *Perception of Self in Emotional Disorder and Psychotherapy.* New York: Plenum Press, 1986.

   Warren H. Jones and Stephen R. Briggs, "The Self-Other Discrepancy in Social Shyness." In R. Schwarzer, ed., *The Self in Anxiety, Stress, and Depression.* Amsterdam: Elsevier, 1984.

 2. Jonathan M. Cheek and Arnold H. Buss, "Shyness and Sociability." *Journal of Personality and Social Psychology,* 41 (1981): 330–339.

   John A. Daly and Laura Stafford, "Correlates and Consequences of Social-Communicative Anxiety." In J. A. Daly and J. C. McCroskey, eds., *Avoiding Communication.* Beverly Hills, CA: Sage Publications, 1984.

 3. Lazaro Garcia and Barry S. Lubetkin, "Clinical Issues in Assertiveness Training with Shy Clients." *Psychotherapy,* 23 (1986): 434–438.

 4. Karen Horney, *Our Inner Conflicts.* New York: W. W. Norton, 1966.

 5. Ian R. H. Falloon, Geoffrey G. Lloyd, and R. Edward Harpin, "The

Treatment of Social Phobia: Real-Life Rehearsal with Nonprofessional Therapists." *Journal of Nervous and Mental Disease,* 169 (1981): 180–184.

6. Gerald M. Phillips, "Rhetoritherapy: The Principles of Rhetoric in Training Shy People in Speech Effectiveness." In W. H. Jones, J. M. Cheek, and S. R. Briggs, eds., *Shyness: Perspectives on Research and Treatment.* New York: Plenum Press. 1986. Adapted by permission of Plenum Press.

7. Valerian J. Derlega, Midge Wilson, and Alan L. Chaikin, "Friendship and Disclosure Reciprocity." *Journal of Personality and Social Psychology,* 34 (1976): 578–582.

8. Warren H. Jones, Steven A. Hobbs, and Don Hockenbury, "Loneliness and Social Skills Deficits." *Journal of Personality and Social Psychology,* 42 (1982): 682–689.

9. See, for example, Don Gabor, *How to Start a Conversation and Make Friends.* New York: Fireside, 1983.

10. See, for example, Alan Garner, *Conversationally Speaking.* New York: McGraw-Hill, 1980. Also Lynne Kelly and Arden K. Watson, *Speaking with Confidence and Skill.* New York: Harper & Row, 1986.

11. Chris L. Kleinke, *Meeting and Understanding People.* New York: W. H. Freeman and Company, 1986. Copyright © 1986 W. H. Freeman and Company. Adapted by permission.

12. Nancy M. Henley, *Body Politics: Power, Sex, and Nonverbal Communication.* Englewood Cliffs, NJ: Prentice-Hall, 1977.
    Mark L. Knapp, *Nonverbal Communication in Human Interaction.* New York: Holt, Rinehart and Winston, 1972.

13. Robert A. Baron, and Donn Byrne, *Social Psychology: Understanding Human Interaction,* 3rd ed. Boston: Allyn and Bacon, 1981.
    Stewart L. Tubbs and Sylvia Moss, *Interpersonal Communication,* 2nd ed. New York: Random House, 1981.

Chapter 6

1. Jonathan M. Cheek, "Shyness," *Encyclopaedia Britannica 1987 Medical and Health Annual.* Chicago: Encyclopaedia Britannica, 1986.
    Ovid Demaris, " 'I Didn't Want to Be Who I Was.' " *Parade Magazine,* July 27, 1986.

Paul Freeman, "Beauty and the Beast Within." *Continental Choice,* January 1988.

Ellen Hawkes, "TV's Golden Girls: They Stir Things Up." *Parade Magazine,* October 26, 1986.

Barbara Leaming, "Orson Welles: The Unfulfilled Promise." *The New York Times Magazine,* July 14, 1985.

Bob Minzesheimer, "They're Pictures of Shyness." *USA Weekend,* June 5–7, 1987.

2. Dan Yakir, "Kaprisky's Lament." *Boston Globe,* May 27, 1987, pages 25 and 30. Reprinted by permission of Dan Yakir.

3. Barbara Powell, *Overcoming Shyness.* New York: McGraw-Hill, 1981.

4. R. T. Santee, and C. Maslach, "To Agree or Not to Agree: Personal Dissent and Social Pressure to Conform," *Journal of Personality and Social Psychology,* 42 (1982): 690–700.

5. "People," *The Boston Globe Magazine,* February 19, 1984.

Chapter 7

1. Virginia P. Richmond, "Implications of Quietness: Some Facts and Speculations." In J. A. Daly and J. C. McCroskey, eds., *Avoiding Communication.* Beverly Hills, CA: Sage Publications, 1984.

Karen S. Rook, "Promoting Social Bonding: Strategies for Helping the Lonely and Socially Isolated." *American Psychologist,* 39 (1984): 1389–1407.

Ladd Wheeler, Harry Reis, and John Nezlek, "Loneliness, Social Interaction, and Sex Roles." *Journal of Personality and Social Psychology,* 45 (1983): 943–953.

Mitchell T. Wittenberg and Harry T. Reis, "Loneliness, Social Skills, and Social Perception." *Personality and Social Psychology Bulletin,* 12 (1986): 121–130.

2. Warren H. Jones and Bruce N. Carpenter, "Shyness, Social Behavior and Relationships." In W. H. Jones, J. M. Cheek, and S. R. Briggs, eds., *Shyness: Perspectives on Research and Treatment.* New York: Plenum Press, 1986.

Ruth Ann Goswick and Warren H. Jones, "Loneliness, Self-Concept, and Adjustment." *Journal of Psychology,* 107 (1981): 237–240.

Helmut Lamm and Stephan Ekkehard, "Loneliness Among German University Students." *Social Behavior and Personality* (in press).

3. Charles G. Lord and Philip G. Zimbardo, "Actor-Observer Differences in the Perceived Stability of Shyness." *Social Cognition,* 3 (1985): 250–265.

Harrison G. Gough and Avril Thorne, "Positive, Negative, and Balanced Shyness: Self-Definitions and the Reactions of Others." In W. H. Jones, J. M. Cheek, and S. R. Briggs, eds., *Shyness: Perspectives on Research and Treatment.* New York: Plenum Press, 1986.

4. Arnold H. Buss, *Social Behavior and Personality.* Hillsdale, NJ: Lawrence Erlbaum Associates, 1986.

5. Joel D. Block, *Friendship.* New York: Collier Books, 1980.

6. Valerian J. Derlega, Midge Wilson, and Alan L. Chaikin, "Friendship and Disclosure Reciprocity." *Journal of Personality and Social Psychology,* 34 (1976): 578–582.

7. Robert A. Baron and Donna Byrne, *Social Psychology: Understanding Human Interaction,* 3rd ed. Boston: Allyn and Bacon, 1981.

8. Educational Exchange of Greater Boston, *Educational Opportunities of Greater Boston for Adults,* 65th annual ed., Catalog No. 65, 1987–1988. Cambridge, MA: 1987.

9. Steve Bhaerman and Don McMillan, *Friends & Lovers: How to Meet the People You Want to Meet.* Cincinnati: Writer's Digest Books, 1986.

Chapter 8

1. Sheila Koren, "The Politics of Shyness: An Uninhibited Review." *State and Mind,* 7 (1979): 30–34.

2. Brian G. Gilmartin, *Shyness and Love: Causes, Consequences, and Treatment.* Lanham, MD: University Press of America, 1987.

3. Hal Arkowitz, Richard Hinton, Joseph Perl, and William Himadi, "Treatment Strategies for Dating Anxiety in College Men Based on Real-Life Practice." *The Counseling Psychologist,* 7 (1978): 41–46.

4. Virginia P. Richmond, "Implications of Quietness: Some Facts and Speculations." In J. A. Daly and J. C. McCroskey, eds., *Avoiding Communication.* Beverly Hills, CA: Sage Publications, 1984.

5. See, for example, Richard Gosse, *Looking for Love in All the Right Places.*

Saratoga, CA: R & E Publishers, 1985. Also Susan Page, *If I'm So Wonderful, Why Am I Still Single?* New York: Viking Press, 1988.

6. Gilmartin, op. cit.

7. Warren Farrell, *Why Men Are the Way They Are.* New York: McGraw-Hill, 1986.

8. Elaine Walster, Jane Allyn Piliavin, and G. William Walster, "The Hard-to-Get Woman." *Psychology Today,* 7 (September 1973): 80–83.

9. Chris L. Kleinke, *Meeting and Understanding People.* New York: W. H. Freeman and Company, 1986. Copyright © 1986 W. H. Freeman and Company. Reprinted with permission.

10. Mark R. Leary, Robin M. Kowalski, and David J. Bergen, "Interpersonal Information Acquisition and Confidence in First Encounters." *Personality and Social Psychology Bulletin,* 14 (1988): 68–77.

11. Andrea M. Carpentieri and Jonathan M. Cheek, "Shyness and the Physical Self: Body Esteem, Sexuality, and Anhedonia." Unpublished manuscript, 1986, Wellesley College, Wellesley, MA 02181.

Lawrence A. Fehr and Leighton E. Stamps, "Guilt and Shyness: A Profile of Social Discomfort." *Journal of Personality Assessment,* 43 (1979): 481–484.

George F. Solomon and Joseph C. Solomon, "Shyness and Sex." *Medical Aspects of Human Sexuality,* May 1971, 10–17.

12. Mark R. Leary and Sharon E. Dobbins, "Social Anxiety, Sexual Behavior, and Contraceptive Use." *Journal of Personality and Social Psychology,* 45 (1983): 1347–1354.

13. A. Caspi, G. Elder, and D. J. Bem, "Moving Away from the World: Life-Course Patterns of Shy Children." *Developmental Psychology,* 24 (1988): 824–831.

Gilmartin, op. cit.

D. P. Wilson, "The Woman Who Has Not Married." *Family Life,* 18 [10] (1958): 1–2.

Chapter 9

1. Lee Iacocca, *Iacocca: An Autobiography.* New York: Bantam Books, 1984.

2. A. Caspi, G. Elder, and D. J. Bem, "Moving Away from the World: Life-Course Patterns of Shy Children." *Developmental Psychology,* 24 (1988): 824–831.

Brian G. Gilmartin, *Shyness and Love: Causes, Consequences, and Treatment.* Lanham, MD: University Press of America, 1987.

D. P. Morris, E. Soroker, and G. Burruss, "Follow-up Studies of Shy, Withdrawn Children—I. Evaluation of Later Adjustment." *American Journal of Orthopsychiatry,* 24 (1954): 743–754.

Sharon Johnson, "The Perils of Shyness on the Job." *The New York Times,* August 1986.

3. Karen L. Kelly, "Shyness and Educational and Vocational Development at Wellesley College." Senior Honors Thesis, Wellesley College, May 1988.

Susan D. Phillips and Monroe A. Bruch, "Shyness and Dysfunction in Career Development." *Journal of Counseling Psychology,* 35 (1988): 159–165.

Virginia P. Richmond, "Implications of Quietness: Some Facts and Speculations." In J. A. Daly and J. C. McCroskey, eds., *Avoiding Communication.* Beverly Hills, CA: Sage Publications, 1984.

4. John A. Daly and James C. McCroskey, "Occupational Desirability and Choice as a Function of Communication Apprehension." *Journal of Counseling Psychology,* 22 (1975) 309–313.

Gilmartin, op. cit.

Johnson, op. cit.

5. Robert O. Hansson, "Shyness and the Elderly." In W. J. Jones, J. M. Cheek, and S. R. Briggs, eds., *Shyness: Perspectives on Research and Treatment.* New York: Plenum Press, 1986.

6. Richard Nelson Bolles, *What Color Is Your Parachute?* Berkeley, CA: Ten Speed Press, 1982.

Richard Nelson Bolles, *The Three Boxes of Life.* Berkeley, CA: Ten Speed Press, 1981.

John L. Holland, *Making Vocational Choices,* 2nd ed. Englewood Cliffs, NJ: Prentice-Hall, 1985.

Barry and Linda Gale, *Discover What You're Best At.* New York: Simon & Schuster, 1986.

7. Richard G. Heimberg, Kevin E. Keller, and Theresa Peca-Baker, "Cognitive Assessment of Social-Evaluative Anxiety in the Job Interview: Job Interview Self-Statement Schedule." *Journal of Counseling Psychology,* 33

(1986): 190–195. Reprinted by permission of the American Psychological Association.

8. Michael T. Motley, "Taking the Terror Out of Talk." *Psychology Today,* 22 (January 1988): 46–49.

Chapter 10

1. Robin Foster Cappe and Lynn E. Alden, "A Comparison of Treatment Strategies for Clients Functionally Impaired by Extreme Shyness and Social Avoidance." *Journal of Consulting and Clinical Psychology,* 54 (1986): 796–801.

   I. R. H. Falloon, P. Lindley, R. McDonald, and I. M. Marks, "Social Skills Training of Outpatient Groups: A Controlled Study of Rehearsal and Homework." *British Journal of Psychiatry,* 131 (1977): 599–609.

   Janet C. Loxley, "Understanding and Overcoming Shyness." In S. Eisenberg and L. E. Patterson, eds., *Helping Clients with Special Concerns.* Boston: Houghton Mifflin, 1979.

   L. Ost, A. Jerremalm, and J. Johansson, "Individual Response Patterns and the Effects of Different Behavioral Methods in the Treatment of Social Phobia." *Behavioral Research and Therapy,* 19 (1981): 1–16.

   Anton Shahar and Michael Merbaum, "The Interaction Between Subject Characteristics and Self-Control Procedures in the Treatment of Interpersonal Anxiety." *Cognitive Therapy and Research,* 5 (1981): 221–224.

   Arden K. Watson, "Alleviation of Communication Apprehension: An Individualized Approach." *Texas Speech Communication Journal,* II (1986): 3–13.

2. Albert Ellis, "The Impossibility of Achieving Consistently Good Mental Health." *American Psychologist,* 42 (April 1987): 364–375.

3. Nikki Meredith, "Testing the Talking Cure." In A. L. Hammond and P. G. Zimbardo, eds., *The Best of Science '80–'86.* Boston: Scott, Foresman, 1988.

4. Steven Starker, "Self-help Treatment Books: The Rest of the Story." *American Psychologist,* 43 (1988): 599–600.

   Bruce A. Thyer, *Treating Anxiety Disorders.* Beverly Hills, CA: Sage Publications, 1987.

5. Martin E. P. Seligman, "Boomer Blues." *Psychology Today,* 22 (October 1988), 50–55.

6. Allan Luks, "Helper's High." *Psychology Today,* 22 (October 1988), 39–42.

Suggested Reading

There are a number of books available for further reading on many of the areas I've discussed. Here are just a few that I've come across and liked.

For additional reading on motivating yourself to change, have a look at one or both of these books:

Alexander, Joe. *Dare to Change*. New York: Signet Books, 1984.
When you're finding it difficult to get yourself to make changes, you may find this book useful. Alexander illustrates how you've learned your present behaviors and how to reprogram yourself for change.

Schmidt, Jerry A. *Help Yourself. A Guide to Self-Change*. Champaign, IL: Research Press, 1976.
This wonderful book focuses on techniques to help yourself change defeating behavior patterns. If you want more help on how to set goals for yourself, this is the book that will help you do just that.

For more on incorporating relaxation techniques into your daily life, here are three suggestions:

Benson, Herbert. *The Relaxation Response.* New York: Avon Books, 1975.

The complete book on learning how to relax. Explains how tension affects our lives and health and why it's so important to take time to relax in our hectic daily lives.

Borysenko, Joan, with Larry Rothstein. *Minding the Body, Mending the Mind.* Reading, MA: Addison-Wesley, 1987.

Borysenko leads readers through the program she cofounded at the Mind/ Body Clinic of New England Deaconess Hospital. Combining relaxation with restructured thinking, Borysenko shows how you can use your mind to improve your health and mental well-being.

Curtis, John D. and Richard A. Detert. *How to Relax.* Palo Alto, CA: Mayfield, 1981.

Curtis and Detert recommend progressive relaxation. Their book goes beyond other relaxation texts with a section entitled "Beyond the Basics." Here they discuss relaxation in the context of everyday activities—walking, standing, talking, and time management.

Do you want more help on boosting your self-esteem? There are seemingly hundreds of books on this topic. Here are just a few:

Branden, Nathaniel. *How to Raise Your Self-Esteem.* New York: Bantam Books, 1987.

Dr. Branden amplifies the theory of self-esteem with action-oriented exercises for building up your self-worth. His book stands out from others by his inclusion of a chapter on nurturing self-esteem in others.

Frey, Diane and C. Jesse Carlock. *Enhancing Self-Esteem.* Muncie, IN: Accelerated Development, Inc., 1984.

Includes theories of self-esteem development, combined with practical exercises you can use to raise your self-esteem. The authors have also devoted chapters to body esteem and women's esteem.

Johnson, Helen M. *How Do I Love Me?,* 2nd ed. Salem, WI: Sheffield Publishing, 1986.

An upbeat and interactive book on raising your self-esteem. A counselor for fifteen years, Helen Johnson approaches her topic with sensitivity and a no-nonsense, can-do flair.

McKay, Matthew and Fanning, Patrick. *Self-Esteem.* New York: St. Martin's Press, 1987.

Many exercises for building self-esteem, including using hypnosis. McKay and Fanning also discuss defenses—behaviors and thoughts that block the growth of self-esteem.

Newman, Mildred and Bernard Berkowitz. *How to Be Your Own Best Friend.* New York: Ballantine Books, 1971.

This little book has sold millions of copies. Comprised of short question-and-answer exchanges, Newman and Berkowitz provide uplifting and thought-provoking "talks" to raise your self-esteem.

If you liked the cognitive approach in Chapter 4, here are two books that use this method exclusively:

Burns, David D. *Feeling Good. The New Mood Therapy.* New York: Signet Books, 1980.

Dr. Burns outlines the principles of cognitive therapy and demonstrates how you can apply them to change your outlook about yourself and your life. Covers boosting your self-esteem, handling criticism, guilt, and overcoming love addiction.

Helmstetter, Shad. *The Self-Talk Solution.* New York: Pocket Books, 1987.

Beyond positive self-statements, self-talk as spelled out here is better described as self-directed talk. Explaining how to incorporate self-talk into your life, Helmstetter covers its applications from relationships to health to work.

As with self-esteem, there is an endless supply of books on social skills. Here are some you may find useful:

Gabor, Don. *How to Start a Conversation and Make Friends.* New York: Fireside Books, 1983.

Conversational do's and don'ts, with a section on improving your ability to remember people's names and "50 Ways to Improve Your Conversation."

Garner, Alan. *Conversationally Speaking.* New York: McGraw-Hill, 1981.

In addition to conversational tips, Garner includes a section on speaking to others in a direct and positive way and how to elicit the same response from them.

Kelly, Lynne and Arden K. Watson. *Speaking with Confidence and Skill.* New York: Harper & Row, 1986.

A terrifically helpful book that incorporates information and guidelines on communicating with instructive exercises. Chapter Two is devoted to determining your strengths and weaknesses as a communicator.

Langdon-Dahm, Martha. *Trade Secrets.* Dayton, OH: Learning Development Systems, Inc., 1986.

Uniquely designed, this book gives "tools" for coping with an enormous variety of social situations. Each tool is defined with an explanation of how it works, examples of situations in which it might be useful, and examples of the technique in action. At the back of the book are tear-out, wallet-sized cards with a summary of each tool.

Meeting new people and forming lasting friendships are the topics of the following books:

Bhaerman, Steve and Don McMillan. *Friends & Lovers: How to Meet the People You Want to Meet.* Cincinnati: Writer's Digest Books, 1986.

Describes strategies for meeting new people and how to develop your own "social agenda." Special chapter on turning acquaintances into friends.

Block, Joel D. *Friendship*. New York: Collier Books, 1980.
   Joel Block conducted a survey on friendship and includes his questionnaire at the beginning of this fine book. He also covers special areas of friendship—within marriage and in the divorce process.

Kleinke, Chris L. *Meeting and Understanding People*. New York: W. H. Freeman and Company, 1986.
   Kleinke reports on the nuts-and-bolts social psychology of everyday interaction with other people. His book includes chapters on nonverbal behavior and how to best present yourself to others.

Pogrebin, Letty Cottin. *Among Friends*. New York: McGraw-Hill, 1987.
   Exquisite book on friends, covering such diverse areas as what constitutes a friendship to fighting with friends and how friendships change throughout our lives.

For further help on establishing a romantic relationship, try one of these books:

Burns, David D. *Intimate Connections*. New York: Signet Books, 1985.
   Step-by-step program for expanding your network of friends and finding an intimate relationship. Includes chapters on sexual relations.

Farrell, Warren *Why Men Are the Way They Are*. New York: McGraw-Hill, 1986.
   A new approach to relationships between men and women that challenges popular assumptions about feminism and sexism. This book gives helpful insights into many aspects of intimate relationships.

Gilmartin, Brian. *Shyness and Love: Causes, Consequences, and Treatment*. Lanham, MD: University Press of America, 1987.
   Gilmartin conducted extensive interviews with 300 extremely love-shy men. His results and recommendations should be informative for men in a similar predicament.

Page, Susan. *If I'm So Wonderful, Why Am I Still Single?* New York: Viking, 1988.

An excellent book that demolishes all the excuses you ever had for being unable to find a mate. Page describes ten practical strategies you can employ to find your way out of the single life.

Every year there's a new book out on how to find and land the best job—check your local bookstore for these. For books that are oriented toward determining your best career choice, and a new one on public speaking, see:

Bolles, Richard. *What Color Is Your Parachute?* Berkeley, CA: Ten Speed Press, 1988.

Updated every year, Bolles gives exercises for helping you find your niche as well as practical advice for job hunting, interviewing, and negotiating salary.

Holland, John L. *Making Vocational Choices,* 2nd ed. Englewood Cliffs, NJ: Prentice-Hall, 1985.

Although targeted at students and professionals, Holland's book includes his widely used vocational interest test as well as a discussion of his theory of personality and work environments, with practical applications.

Sarnoff, Dorothy. *Never Be Nervous Again.* New York: Crown, 1987.

The definitive book on preparing a public speech from start to finish. Sarnoff incorporates the technical aspects of preparing and delivering a presentation with techniques to chase away the jitters.

If you have suggestions for improving a future edition of this book, you may write me at the following address:

Professor Jonathan Cheek
Department of Psychology
Wellesley College
Wellesley, MA 02181

Index